Human Services in the Age of New Technology

04/18.

Public Policy and Social Welfare
A Series Edited by Bernd Marin

 European Centre Vienna

Volume 20

David Phillips, Yitzhak Berman

Human Services in the Age of New Technology

Harmonising Social Work and Computerisation

Avebury

Aldershot · Brookfield USA · Hong Kong · Singapore · Sydney

Published by
Avebury
Ashgate Publishing Limited
Gower House
Croft Road
Aldershot
Hants GU11 3HR
England

Ashgate Publishing Company
Old Post Road
Brookfield
Vermont 05036
USA

Composition: Michael Eigner
European Centre for Social Welfare Policy and Research
Berggasse 17
1090 Vienna
Austria

British Library Cataloguing-in-Publication Data. A catalogue record for this book is available from the British Library.

ISBN 1-85972-128-1

Printed by Druck Partner Rübelmann, Germany.

to our wives
Jane and Bryna

Contents

Acknowledgements   ix

Preface   xi

PART I: GENERAL ISSUES   1

Chapter 1   Problems of the Past and Issues for the Future   3

Chapter 2   People and Computers in Social Work Agencies   31

PART II: CONCEPTUAL, ORGANISATIONAL
              AND POLICY ISSUES   47

Chapter 3   IT and Social Work: Conceptual Issues   49

Chapter 4   IT and the Social Work Agency:
            Organisational and Management Issues   67

Chapter 5   Policy Issues   81

PART III: IT IN PRACTICE   95

Chapter 6   Issues in the Implementation of IT   97

Chapter 7   IT in Action in the Social Services   113

Epilogue   135

Bibliography   137

Acknowledgements

The authors met for the first time at a conference in Jerusalem in 1989 organized jointly by the European Centre for Social Welfare Policy and Research and the Israel Ministry of Labour and Social Affairs. Here the seed of the idea for the book was sown. We owe a great debt to Dr Patrick Kenis of the European Centre who gave us encouragement and offered us help.

Two of our friends, Jeong Hwa Kim, research student at Sheffield University, and Dr A. Solomon Eaglstein, Director of Research, Israel Ministry of Labour and Social Affairs, read and made trenchant critical comments on an early draft of the book. The book is much improved because of their selfless efforts.

Sol Eaglstein deserves a second mention. We wrote this book almost entirely via email between Sheffield and Jerusalem and Sol acted as the Jerusalem postmaster for over a year until Yitzhak Berman's modem was up and running. This was an immensely time-consuming task.

Dr Monica Shapira has graciously permitted us to make extensive use of her work on the Juvenile Probation Decision Support System. Yehoshafat Harel, Director, Division of Research, Planning and Training, Ministry of Labour and Social Affairs, enabled Yitzhak Berman to work on the manuscript as part of his workload.

We also gratefully acknowledge the following for their help:
- Chaim Jutkowitz for carrying out a literature review in the early stages of the project.
- Dr Duncan Matheson, School of Social Work, Laurentian University, for permission to quote from his paper "Innovative Use of Computers for Planning in Human Service Organizations", paper prepared for the Second Human Service Information Technology Applications (HUSITA-2) International Conference, New Brunswick, New Jersey, June 26-30, 1991.

- Marvin Ishai of the Division of Research, Planning and Training, Ministry of Labour and Social Affairs, Jerusalem, for listening to "new" ideas.
- The British Council for funding Yitzhak Berman's trip to the UK in order to complete the writing of this book.
- The Centre for Human Services, University of Southampton for permission to use material from the journal *New Technology in the Human Services*, 'A Decision Support System in Resource Allocation: the Political Process in Rational Decision Making', 1992, 6 (1): 8-14.

Preface

Social work has a professional identity and value base. Simultaneously, in organisational terms its operation is normally subjugated within a hierarchical, line management structure and it has to perform agency functions – often statutory in nature – which are not fully in accord with its humanistic vocational and professional identity. This establishes a potential tension, almost a power struggle, between agency function and professional integrity.

The ethos of the agencies as distributors of social welfare services can be seen to be humanistic in an equitable, fair and even-handed way. The ethos of social work as a profession is founded upon respect for the individual, on non-judgementalism and on positive, unconditional regard. These values can, of course, be complementary but they can also be in competition with each other. If there is conflict then the introduction of information technology (IT) can lead to serious difficulties. Computerised information systems can change the balance of power in organisations; and in social services agencies they often tilt the balance of power emphatically towards management. This can lead to a serious reduction in social worker autonomy.

But the problems are not only about raw power. They go to the heart of the identity of social work. Of all the professions – with the notable exception of the priesthood – social work is the one which is most pastoral and person-oriented. Its essence resides in respect for the individual human being, her or his uniqueness and humanity. Common sense perceptions of computers do not rest easily with this ethos. Computers seem to signify all that is non-human and their defining characteristics (such as logical structures, electronic circuitry, mechanistic processing) are the antithesis of the defining characteristics of social work – compassion, unconditional positive regard and empathy.

One of our aims in this book is to counter that common sense perception and to demonstrate that computers, if appropriately used, can be a major asset to even the most individualistic and person-centred social worker. Moreover, social workers do not have to make compromises or change their occupational practices in order for their work to be enhanced by IT.

Until recently this has not been readily apparent. The fact that the nature of social work itself is not at first sight easily amenable to computerisation has led to exasperation amongst information technology innovators whose conceptual frameworks are embedded in the technology rather than in social work. As a result some commentators assert that effective computerisation requires social workers to make fundamental shifts in how they think about cases, observe clients and record clinical events (Gripton, Licker and de Groot, 1988).

Given this sorry state of affairs it is perhaps fortunate that even in this last decade of the twentieth century social work has so far been little affected by IT. Most of the developments to date, even the most effective and widely accepted applications, have been specifically oriented to the needs of social services management rather than to the delivery of social work services. Applications of direct and explicit benefit to the social service process – to the worker-client interface – and therefore of direct and tangible benefits to the clients themselves, have not been particularly successful. They tended to get stuck at the prototype stage – or even earlier – through lack of support.

The main purpose of this book is to spread the word about the immense potential of computerisation to enhance the service provided for their clients by social workers. But this does not mean that the book is brim-full of good news. Part of the message needs to be cautionary – about the possibility of computerisation damaging social work, and how to avoid that.

Part I of the book sets the scene. The first chapter discusses the reasons why computerisation has been so unsuccessful in the past. Then it explores a range of issues which need to be addressed in the future if computerisation is to be successful. At a conceptual level these include professional, organisational and ideological issues, while at the practical end they include the response of service users. In Chapter 2 we look, perhaps a little tongue-in-cheek, at personal responses to computerisation amongst social workers, from the blatant Luddite to the utter fanatic. We then investigate different responses from social work agencies, from a total absence or tokenistic response at one extreme through to complete integration and innovative responses at the other. The chapter concludes with a survey of studies of social work computerisation in practice.

Part II deals with conceptual, organisational and policy issues. Chapter 3 tackles two difficult issues: identity and education. What is IT? What is social work? And what is the relationship – or range of relationships – between them? We do not pretend to have found a definitive answer to these imponderable questions but we hope that we have shed some light on them. Perhaps the most important factor in the future of social work, and of the part IT will have to play in it, is social work education. We nail our colours to the mast and unequivocally support those educationalists who are endeavouring to imbue social work IT teaching with a humanistic rather than a technological ethos.

Chapter 4 briefly dips its toe into organisational theory and then explores the difficulties and contradictions of computerising a hybrid, part rational, part natural systems organisational structure. Policy issues are explored in Chapter 5, which commences with a discussion of the policy process. This is followed by an analysis of the IT-oriented policy of "care management". A case-study of power politics and IT implementation gives a vivid example of the issues at stake.

Part III is explicitly practical. Chapter 6 deals with the implementation of information technology in the social services. We concentrate very much on what management needs to do in order to ensure smooth implementation and commissioning of major systems. The focus quickly moves to front line workers because our fundamental message is that of staff involvement. We also explore issues of resource requirements and information needs.

Chapter 7 looks at IT in action in the social services. Unlike other texts on computerisation of social work it does not deal with management systems but explicitly explores IT innovations of direct use to social work practice which are up and running and of demonstrable benefit. Readers are introduced to social work information, decision support and expert systems.

Finally in an epilogue we present our own personal recipe for a value orientation which will facilitate the effective implementation of IT in social work.

Spring 1995   David Phillips (Sheffield)
                                                        Yitzhak Berman (Jerusalem)

PART I

GENERAL ISSUES

CHAPTER 1

Problems of the Past and Issues for the Future

The history of computerisation of the social services is one full of false dawns and drama. So far no-one has attempted to provide definitive documentation of the early days of information technology (IT) in social work. Sadly, it is not our purpose to do so – the story is fascinating but is too long to be told here. What we will do in this chapter is introduce the reader to some of the major reasons why social services computerisation has taken place so slowly and to address some of the important issues for the future.

Reasons for Underdevelopment

First we need to see just how far behind social work is in computing compared to the business world and to other professions. Caputo in his important and influential book asserts witheringly that "the first 30 years of computer use have already left the human services a score or two behind industry and business and, though to a lesser degree, health and education" (1988: 5). Given that two score is 40 years he is obviously making extensive use of poetic licence. He is joined by Cnaan who goes even further: "If the social welfare field is decades behind the business world in the more mundane aspects of computerization of role tasks, it is light years behind in even conceiving of the use of computers to facilitate service provision" (1989a: 2).

So the social services are a long way behind the competition. Why is this? Caputo (1988) claims that cost used to be a major reason, but with the recent dramatic reduction of the price of computing power this can no longer be the fundamental barrier it used to be. His other major explanation is lack of knowledge about the usefulness of computers, a problem that has been addressed only within the past 10 years. Cnaan is in accord with Caputo in specifying ignorance about the usefulness of IT as a major problem, particularly in relation to what he calls the profession's most sacred domain – direct practice: "Questions as to whether the new technologies can affect or modify direct practice or clinical work, and whether these effects will be advantageous to clients have yet to be answered, either in the literature, or in social work practice itself" (Cnaan, 1989a: 2).

The reasons for this state of affairs are deep-rooted and relate to different spheres of action: social work as a professional and organisational activity; the identity, attitudes and perceptions of social workers; organisational structures and agency functions; and research, development, education and dissemination.

Social Work and Social Workers

The Nature of Social Work

The computerisation of large-scale routinised activities is difficult enough, but it is nowhere near as difficult as computerising social work. The social work task is complex, multidimensional and is difficult, perhaps even impossible, to systematise. Thus at best, the introduction of IT into social work is a major challenge.

The flexibility and the individualised interaction which is so characteristic of social work is cited by Glastonbury, LaMendola and Toole (1988) as the most crucial *technical* reason for the present underdevelopment of IT in social work. The intellectual and decision-making currency of the social services is the discursive narrative, whether it be in face to face discussion in a case conference, case notes, court reports, or in consultations with clients. Finding a way for computer-based applications to deal effectively with this medium is a major problem in the development of IT expertise. On the one hand we have a profession which has a knowledge base and decision-making system predicated upon practice wisdom (in non-codified natural language). On the other hand there is a technology which can be of assistance if the information it uses is structured and codified.

Even more problematic than this is the nature of the organisational environment within which social work operates. Social services organisations are different to other organisations on three counts. First, they serve clients who bring with them unique problems each needing individualised and increasingly holistic responses. Secondly the social services are interorganisational in nature; and thirdly their organisational environment is dynamic and changing at such a pace that recording it is nearly impossible (Caputo, 1988).

Caputo's second point is given heavy emphasis by Schoech and Schkade (1980a). They predict that the lack of integrated service delivery systems and the interorganisational nature of the social services will slow down IT implementation. Whereas people's needs for social care may well be indivisible, the services whose duty it is to meet them are fragmented; they cross administrative boundaries within and between national, regional and local state, voluntary and private sectors. Co-ordination of information between a multiplicity of machines, information systems and administrative boundaries is so problematical that it can be easier to do it manually than by machine. In parentheses it has to be added that communications interfaces are the Achilles heel of the futuristic century world of IT – getting two different computers to talk to each other *ought* to be easy, but we still have not got it fully cracked.

There is some good news on this front, though. By dint of much consultation and forward planning a uniform computerised client intake form is being shared by 275 social service agencies in one county in North Carolina (Highfill et al., 1986). And Arno Penzias, Nobel prize winner and world expert on IT, predicts that within the next five years a "seamless interface" between all machines will be developed (Penzias, 1993).

Schoech and Schkade (1980a) identify another problem – that of measuring the outputs and outcomes of social work interventions. They cite the difficulty of developing measurable units of service for defining social work outputs and the impacts these may have on clients. These difficulties are related both to technical problems of quantifying services and to political problems of constantly changing goals, mandates and emphases inherent in our democratic system of planning.

Difficult though those issues are, Schoech and Schkade dramatically underestimate the extent and nature of the problem. It is not just an issue of *measurement* it is more of a problem of *identification* of outputs and even knowledge in social work. Caputo reminds us that social service organisations lack determinate and effective technologies. He claims that most social service methods are based on limited and fragmentary knowledge bases, and that few can be shown to be effective. As a result, he claims, social work organisations develop ideological systems in place of knowledge systems to legitimate professional actions. Thus "the creation and development of explicit criteria for performance assessment and measures of accountability become highly problematic" (Caputo, 1988: 72). This problematic knowledge base for social work has posed major difficulties and will continue to do so.

No matter what its problems are in relation to a knowledge base, social work does possess a firm value base. This too has hindered computerisation. Pardeck, Umfress and Murphy (1990) identify problems associated with the value base of social work. They remind us that the profession is based predominantly on humanistic values which require a client-centred orientation. They claim that an ideology has emerged which suggests that computers are intrinsically harmful to clients. They may be overstating their case here. Williams and Forrest (1988) from their meticulous empirical study, agree that social workers' reactions to office automation and management information systems are often largely negative, but they come to different conclusions about its causality. Instead of talking about emergent ideologies they hypothesise that the problem lies primarily in the difficulty of integrating new technology into the culture and routines of social work practice. This can be compounded by fear and ignorance of the unknown, embarrassment or indignity of making mistakes, distrust over reliability and accuracy, jargon, and issues of confidentiality.

Practitioner Resistance

Resistance to new technology amongst workers is not unique to social work – on the contrary it is near universal at least as an initial reaction. But practitioner resistance in the social services has some special features. We deal briefly first with personal responses to professional issues. Williams and Forrest (1988) found in their research that the normal worries most people experience when they first use computers were not the main cause of the hostility which emerged. It was due to the fact that in their study (and in most other initial implementation situations) the computers were being used for management information systems which the practitioners perceived as both an irritant which would not benefit them at all and as a threat to their professional autonomy.

Lohmann and Wolvovski as long ago as 1979 pointed to an intra-professional tension which had then recently emerged but has since become a bigger problem. They found that the professionals who were most knowledgeable and sophisticated in computer usage were those with a quantitatively oriented "scientific" approach to social work who wanted to use computers to clean up "all the messy, sloppy, qualitative thinking they thought they saw". Even though their tongues were firmly in their cheeks in this passage they touched a raw nerve. Social work is still recovering from the over-zealous, insensitive and often inappropriate attempts made by that first generation of social service computer innovators in the 1970s and 1980s.

With true social work insight Bronson, Pelz and Trzcinski stress the importance of agency atmosphere in accounting for resistance to the technology: "When the internal atmosphere is warm – supportive, trusting and cooperative – the staff will most likely respond in a similar way to the introduction of computers. On the other hand, when there is a chill in the air – conflict, distrust, or discontent – staff resistance is probable" (1988: 64).

Moving on to more general issues, Lamb (1990) specifies four possible reasons for practitioner resistance to computerisation: a perception that learning to use computers is more trouble than it is worth; lack of mathematical orientation amongst social service staff; a paucity of examples of successful integration of computers into the social services; and a lack of understanding of the capability of computers to enhance practice. Hammer and Hile (1985) report on a major review of literature on resistance amongst mental health professionals to computerisation. They identify a series of structural and process variables at the individual, group and environmental level, including: presumed client resistance; goal conflict; evaluation of practitioners' work; client confidentiality; and organisational change. They rehearse many of the arguments we will meet later, for example: initial involvement of practitioners in the computerisation process is important; hardware acquisition can be traumatic – computerisation takes a long time and needs to be fitted into agency work cycles; training and good documentation are crucially important; and computers have an impact upon agencies which leads to organisational change. This last point is potentially of considerable importance.

Moving from this synoptic, "shopping list" approach to the other end of the spectrum, Smith and Bolitho (1989) put forward a unique and intriguing proposition about a possible major cause of practitioner resistance to IT – that of the transformation of the nature of *information* itself by new technology. They believe that social workers' resistance to IT arises from a confusion over the nature of "information". They suggest that this confusion is a consequence of social work education and socialisation which does not seriously consider the nature and use of information in the provision of competent professional practice. They then make a very telling point: "Contrast the present inattention to information with the value given to 'communication' as a substantive area of professional social work education. Communication as a topic is covered in numerous practical contexts such as in interpersonal and group skills teaching, and in formal academic content, as part of principles of practice" (Smith and Bolitho, 1989: 86-87).

At first sight this argument may seem rather esoteric, but it does chime in with the line developed by LaMendola (1987). It nevertheless is probably true to say that they overstate their case. One needs only to look at the elements of social work curricula which deal with statutory obligations and legal aspects of social work practice, particularly in the vexed areas of child abuse and mental health work, to become aware that information in the form of evidence, legal requirements etc. looms large in social work education. The issue at stake here is that new technology can unleash a torrent of information, transforming it from a rare and relatively precious but homely commodity into one which is ubiquitous but esoteric, sometimes worthless, sometimes apparently sinister.

Organisation and Management

Schoech and Schkade (1980a) give a persuasive explanation for the lack of further development of IT in the social services beyond its initial tentative implementation. They postulate that the growth curve of IT implementation is very steep at the early stages but slows down as the IT system approaches maturity: "This is an evolutionary process requiring considerable learning and adaptation on the part of the agency. Changes in this stage cannot be rushed: the information system must be revised and adapted until it fits the organisation" (1980a: 22). They seem to get the right answer, but perhaps for the wrong reason. Surely what is important here is the issue of the "organised anarchy" of social service agencies rather than issues of system maturity.

Gandy and Tepperman also report that computerisation has not lived up to its promises. They write rather ruefully: "Organisations introduced computers believing that they would provide greater efficiency. We found no evidence that the promise of greater efficiency has been realised in any of the eight organisations we studied" (1990: 181). The reasons for this make a sad litany: first, most of these organisations were computerised without clear goals; second. staff were not involved in planning or implementing the new system; third, senior staff often failed to give leadership; fourth, the agencies were unwilling to use the technology in ways that could be perceived as changing established procedures, staff relationships or organisational structure; and finally, they were not effectively resourced. The following problems and issues were mentioned most frequently by staff: "(1) a lack of confidence in the accuracy of computer generated data; (2) the failure of computerization to increase productivity; (3) the increase in paperwork associated with the computerization; (4) additional costs of computerization to the organization; and (5) limited participation of direct service and support staff in planning for and implementing computerization" (ibid.: 182).

This is all gloomy stuff: in these agencies it looks as though computerisation was not actually a disaster, but it was not much use either. As we will see in Chapter 4, they made a series of recommendations for improving things. For the moment, though, we will leave them with these rather lugubrious conclusions:

> For the time being, computer use is limited and easily avoided within the organizations we studied. The computer has had little impact, either positive or negative. For most, it is a gadget, a new toy that adorns the organization without hurting or helping. The motivation to make it more than that is, apparently, lacking at all levels of the organization (ibid.: 183).

Research, Education and Development

Pardeck, Umfress and Murphy (1990) review research studies which claim that computers are typically used within social work agencies by only a small number of administrative staff for information management. There are some newer implementations (initial interview, clinical testing, diagnosis and consulting) but only a small number of agencies seem to be using this technology. Pardeck et al. cite three factors to explain this: first, that very little has been published in the professional social work literature; second, little is being done about computerisation in social work education; and thirdly, a lack of effective research.

Gandy and Tepperman's review of the literature similarly concludes that there is a paucity of information on the impact of computerisation. They tell us they were unable to locate good research on the effectiveness of these new systems and they identify two problem areas which they claim characterise the present state of knowledge and empirical research on computerisation in social work:

1) Shortage of careful empirical research, coupled with considerable speculative, prescriptive and normative debate which is not empirically grounded.
2) Lack of a consistent picture in the published empirical research of the reasons for computerisation or its consequences.

It is important to note that it is not just empiricist or positivist researchers who demand that judgements on the success or otherwise of computerisation be grounded in empirical findings. For example, Karger and Kreuger, whose work is at a high level of sociological abstraction, insist that: "an examination of the effects of computers in the social service workplace must be based on present technology, and reflect the experiences of human service workers who encounter these machines" (1988: 114). They remind us too that most of what is known about the effects of technology is based on survey research of dubious quality and impressionistic observations.

Pardeck, Umfress and Murphy (1990) explore the issue of emphasis in social work education: "Emphasis can be placed on either the logistics or the philosophy of computerisation. At this time, the focus appears to be on the mastery of technique, and as long as this is the case, insight into how computers can be used in a socially sensitive manner will probably not be acquired". In Chapter 3 we explore issues relating to computers in social work education in more depth. Our conclusion is that Pardeck et al. conceptualise the debate too narrowly. It is necessary to go beyond the philosophy of computerisation: it is important to situate discussion of IT in social work within a *humanistic*, not a *technological* framework.

As a computer enthusiast himself, Glastonbury (1988) poses the uncomfortable question "Is it all really worth it?" and he suggests several uncomfortable answers. He concludes that it is difficult to disagree with the argument that enhanced social work efficiency would be achieved: "if IT investment was kept to word processing and client indexing, and the rest of the money spent on employing more social workers, psychologists and other social services staff ... IT today and yesterday has only shown flashes of its real capability: it flourishes in the human services in the promise of tomorrow. There are limits to the credibility of a technology which seems perpetually unable to deliver the goods today" (Glastonbury, 1988: 187).

But Now for Some Good News: Learning from Other People's Mistakes

Learning from one's own mistakes is often unavoidable, but the smart thing to do is to learn from mistakes made by other people. Because of its late start, the social work sector is in a perfect position to avoid some of the errors made in the business world. It is certainly true that the uniqueness of social work as a profession will lead to some singular problems not experienced in other areas, but the vast majority of possible mistakes and problems will have been encountered already. As early as 1980, Schoech and Schkade wrote an article entitled "What Human Services can Learn from Business about Computing" in which they offer us the following comforting advice:

> While a human service agency can purchase sophisticated DP [data processing] technologies, it still must go through the long, tedious, and frustrating process of adapting the DP system to the organisation and the user if the system is to be successful. While the adjustment of the DP system to the organisation and the user is a process that cannot be purchased or rushed, human service administrators have a tremendous potential advantage because they can benefit from lessons learned the hard way in business (Schoech and Schkade, 1980a: 18).

Major Issues for the Future

The explanation for the present restricted development of computers in the social services lies in the past. If IT is to be used more effectively in the future then several important issues need to be addressed.

Philosophical Issues

The philosophical debate around computerisation has in general not been very edifying. Some bright spots, some shafts of illumination have shone through, but for the most part a fog has descended upon the debate – a fog of inarticulate imprecision and near-banality, sometimes enlivened (though not illuminated) by the battle cries of the different protagonists. In one ear we hear prophesies of doom from commentators with a fear of change verging on that of the dark ages and critics with a suspicion of novelty worthy of Galileo's inquisitors. In the other ear we hear shouts of "Eureka!" from computer evangelists who tell us to cast off the antediluvian shackles of human thinking and to embrace the new, transcendental epistemology of the IT age. The one point of agreement amongst the most vociferous protagonists – whether they be for or against the New Technology – is the claim that it is not merely a neutral, value-free tool. Many of the commentators oversimplistically assume that a monolithic and unchangeable value set is indelibly associated with IT. Where they disagree is whether or not they approve of these values and in which direction they might lead social work.

The purportedly value-laden nature of IT is a theme which recurs under many different guises throughout the literature. In particular it emerges in discussions of ideological, professional and organisational issues. In addition to any intrinsic properties of IT, Christensen (1986) reminds us emphatically that technological decisions contain a moral dimension.

The most prolific contributors to the anti-IT school are John Murphy and John Pardeck, along with their associates. Over the past decade they have built up a substantial, though often florid, critique, the core of which at least merits serious attention. To start at the most abstract level, they claim that the values of IT lead to a "computer-culture" and "technological world-view". They argue that computers differ from other tools in that they are not passive, that computer technology participates actively in shaping its own environment. Even more fundamentally, it is claimed that there is a danger of IT obscuring the human context into which it is introduced (Murphy and Pardeck, 1988).

In a later publication they present a "conceptual underside", a "world-view" embodying assumptions which require that reality be construed in a way that may undermine the delivery of social services. They argue further that modern society has become enslaved by technology and that the techno-rationality of the computer is seen as dictating working environments and conceptions of what is correct or even possible to achieve (Murphy and Pardeck, 1990a). This is all heady stuff: indeed, some of it is "head in the clouds" stuff. There are esoteric issues here which would merit attention in a philosophy text. For our more down-to-earth purposes the crucial message relates to the danger of reality being reconstructed and constrained in a mechanistic way which limits the provision of social services.

One of their most telling points is that there is a real danger of the usurping of vital but non-numeric qualitative knowledge by quantification. Taken to extremes, this can lead to the imposition of a mechanistic "knowledge-base" which through its inability to handle "soft" data excludes nonquantifiable knowledge or information and thus transforms (some would say it subverts) the foundations of social work decision-making and knowledge (Murphy, Pardeck, Nolan and Pilotta, 1987).

There is another danger in relation to quantification – that of the mis-codification of nonnumeric data. Murphy and Pardeck are particularly concerned with the problems computers may encounter in coping with the linguistic subtleties of everyday natural language: "Without really understanding how language is used, behaviour is arbitrarily labelled. As a result, not only may a client's predicament be seriously misconstrued, he or she may be permanently stigmatised" (Murphy and Pardeck, 1986). But it is not just mis-codification. There are important moral principles at stake here too, particularly related to the dangers highlighted by Weizenbaum as long ago as 1976, when he expressed his fears about use of the programme he had designed ("ELIZA") to perform non-directive therapy along Rogerian lines. But the programme in reality only mimicked the therapy he was trying to emulate. Hence Weizenbaum's famous nostrum that "respect, understanding and love are not technical problems".

Somewhat more controversially Murphy and Pardeck assert that "the computer micro-world is able to create the illusion that computers generate information untrammelled by situational exigencies ... The computer micro-world, because it is sustained by judgements that are presumed to be universally acceptable, is able to lull persons into believing that opinion can be separated from fact" (Murphy and Pardeck, 1990b: 68). The fact-value debate is bread-and-butter for undergraduate social science seminars but the issues of "untrammelled information" is of more substantive import. Smith and Bolitho (1989) have a very different perspective: They criticise many social work professionals for assuming "that technology generates value-laden information instead of accepting that the concept has a highly specialised specific connotation in its proper technological context" (p. 86).

Murphy and Pardeck's main concern, though, is not the overt misuse of technology. They claim that the integrity of clients can be routinely violated by the *correct* use of computers: "In short, a client can be misclassified, misunderstood, and thus made to conform to standards that have no relevance ... Under the guise of science, erroneous judgements may be made regularly about clients ... Clients are thus at risk of being violated by computerization" (Murphy and Pardeck, 1990b: 72). Here they undo much of the good work they have done. They rightly warn us that faulty conceptualisation can cause ethical problems, that computers can subtly alter therapy and that errors and misclassifications can have serious consequences. But they spoil their case by overstating it. Instead of just claiming that these sorts of problems are *possible* (a proposition with which few would disagree) they slip into the assumption that they are *inevitable*.

Karger and Kreuger explore some more fertile philosophical areas but unfortunately display the same tendency towards overstatement as do Murphy and Pardeck. They explore the effects computers have on our conception of time. Computers routinely on a day-by-day basis achieve tasks impossible to a human in a lifetime. They claim that the perceived time-efficiency in an IT-dominated social service agency will lead to unintended and profound consequences for social work: "The temporal plasticity characteristic of human service interviews begins to be viewed as badly managed time, as the desultory nature of an interview begs to be rationalized" (1988: 118). They use a similar argument in relation to intersubjectivity – people are sociable and intersubjective: computers impose a solitary isolated mode of discourse. Their logic is faultless if what they are saying is that computerisation can lead to these unfortunate results. Here, however, they are putting an inflexible case: they are telling us that computerisation *does* lead to these results.

It has to be said that there are plenty of commentators holding equally problematical views at the opposite end of the spectrum – in defence of the computer worldview. Most of these, however, declaim their views in a less abstract and philosophical manner, and we will meet a representative sample of them (see e.g. the quote from Brinckmann on p. 16). One major task for social philosophers which needs to be undertaken is the rigorous exploration of the philosophical implications of IT in social work, with particular reference to issues of value. Meanwhile, we will move away from these more esoteric fields.

Ethical Issues

Frederic Reamer, in a paper directly addressing ethical dilemmas in implementing new technologies in social work, asserts that the technology in itself is neutral. He highlights human volition and motivations in its implementation and use: "Clearly technology in itself is neither good nor bad, but depends for its virtue on the ethical choices of those who control it. In the careless hands of those who fail to grasp the nature of moral questions, the most benign form of technology can lead to unspeakable harm. In the cautious hands of conscientious professionals it has the impressive capacity to enhance the lives of the people we aim to help" (1986: 471). He claims that the emergence of new technology provides a mixed blessing for social work. It brings a collection of moral puzzles that were unknown to previous generations of practitioners and leads to ethical questions that permeate service delivery at all levels in the social services and for all client groups.

Terry Holbrook gives a graphic example of just the sort of misuse of IT which Reamer was referring to:

> Not long ago I read a newspaper story about a social worker, employed by the Welfare Fraud Division of a local Department of Social Services. According to the article, while the worker was on his lunch hour, he saw an attractive young woman, driving a Mercedes. He took down her licence number, went back to his office, and using his desk-top computer called up on his screen the young woman's vital statistics from the department of Motor Vehicles. With her social security number, address, birthdate, and a phoney case record number, he was able to find out from various data banks at his disposal (he had to wait one full day for data from the I.R.S. [Inland Revenue Service]) the woman's marital status, alimony, property, interest income, number of dependants, and, among other things, the fact she had a learning disabled son. He later contacted the woman, posing as an expert on the learning disabled (1990: 107).

This is a clear example of the ability of computers to engender qualitative changes in social environments. But it is not the machines which he is blaming. He strongly maintains that it is people who are in control of these machines. Therefore practitioners have a responsibility to keep clients fully appraised of the extent of computerised information relating to their cases and the steps taken to protect it. He then goes on to defend the security of computerised data by pointing out that computers generally require security clearances and passwords, whereas manual systems usually only require a single signature on routine request. He accepts that instantaneous access to computerised confidential information is readily available to people who know how to work the system but claims, perhaps somewhat optimistically, that the chances of detection are higher in a computerised system.

Many other commentators take the same line. Watson, for example, underlines Holbrook's emphasis on the human rather than the technical threat to privacy. He insists that: "The existence of computerized information itself poses no threat to privacy. The threat arises, as ever, from *people* and the use they might make of the scale and range of the computer's capabilities". He supports this radical claim by saying that advances in IT *in themselves* do not threaten our moral commitments, but that they do provide a new context within which their commitments must be addressed. He then makes the important point that the major threat comes from people who are authorised users, as well as from people who are not, and with this in mind he enjoins us to ask "who has the right to know what, and about whom" (Watson, 1989: 154).

Lamb goes even further and claims that confidentiality as an ethical issue "seems to be resolved today, at least in the literature if not in the minds of practitioners, with the knowledge that computer files can be made safer and more secure than the central office file cabinet" (1990: 32). Although these comments provide a useful counterbalance to some of the more sensationalist scare stories which abound, nevertheless they all seem to be playing down the real and new security problems which emerge with the advent of computerised databases and networks.

None of these commentators, though, take account of the increase in scale of the problem. Several thousand case records can be downloaded in minutes onto diskettes which fit comfortably into a jacket pocket, whereas the theft of a similar number of manual files would take hours and a pick-up truck.

A classic example of this was revealed in *Newsweek* in September 1992 which tells the astonishing story of Charles Hayes, a dealer who bid $45 for some used U.S. government computer equipment. He got more than he bargained for, though. The computers held lists of confidential informants held by the U.S. Justice Department for federal criminal investigations and the names of people in the federal witness protection programme, people whose lives depended on their whereabouts not falling into the wrong hands. By the time the mistake was spotted though, he had already sold the computers again (de Silva, 1992).

Many commentators play down such events as "scare stories" and prefer to see the problems in terms of the fears of over-anxious practitioners rather than reflecting objective reality. Hammer and Hile (1985) point out that, although automated systems may be at least as safe if not safer than traditional systems, they are not perceived to be so by many practitioners, for whom this is a "red flag" issue. Glastonbury (1985) reported that a general concern amongst respondents to a survey on confidentiality was that the very existence of computerised information posed a serious threat to privacy. Macarov (1990) raises similar issues and he wisely advises us to keep a close watch on the qualitative changes which can occur in the security of confidential client records as a result of changes in technology.

Erdman and Foster also deal with this point in their study of the ethics of the direct assessment of clients. They raise a wide range of ethical issues, including those relating to differential results pertaining to disadvantaged groups. Their overall conclusions from their review of this literature were positive, subject to some qualifications. They concluded that many of the ethical concerns associated with computer use disappear upon close examination and that computer applications offer many advantages to the practitioner. There is one dark cloud on their horizon, though. They invoke the spectre of the two-way television in George Orwell's *1984* in their discussion of "omnipresent evaluation " – the capacity of the computerised Big Brother to be watching us all the time: "Such capabilities already exist, as computers are now used by some employers to conduct job evaluations" (Erdman and Foster, 1988: 84). They find this to be a disturbing precedent because the increase in jobs involving direct computer interaction gives greater opportunity for computer monitoring and control of workers' activity. They accept that accountability for work performance is a legitimate goal, but claim that "omnipresent surveillance" should be limited to extreme cases in a democratic society. They feel that the problem is exacerbated by the fact that data can be collected without an individual's knowledge or permission.

These concerns about professionals' work being evaluated are echoed by Hammer and Hile (1985) who attribute much practitioner resistance to a desire to maintain autonomy and avoid direct evaluation. They are borne out, too, in Vafeas' study. When he introduced a computerised case management system there were initial concerns among workers about client confidentiality but these soon faded away and were replaced by more pressing concerns. The system helped the workers to identify their mistakes and omissions more easily than they could when using a manual system, but their supervisors too could do the same. He reported that the workers felt uncomfortable with aspects of the system which made their problems more transparent (Vafeas, 1991).

So the overall conclusions from these sources are that: first, confidentiality is a genuine issue, but most commentators think it can be kept under control by rigorous safety checks and constant vigilance; and secondly that there are new opportunities for practitioner evaluation and monitoring by managers through computer systems which can affect workers' autonomy. The commentators here believe that there is no need for panic or undue anxiety because these are not revolutionary, new or cataclysmic problems. But there is cause for concern and vigilance because the power of computers adds a new facet to problems of which we are already aware.

Social Responsibility Issues

We have already discussed social responsibility in relation to the duty of social services agencies to ensure confidentiality of their computerised records. But there is a wider issue at stake as well, in which social work can play a more positive role. This relates to the conception of social work as a positive force within society enabling disadvantaged people to gain equitable access to societal resources and life chances. More fundamentally it is to do with the role of social work in empowering disadvantaged people. Cnaan, who has fought unrelentingly to remind the social work profession of its obligations in this area, classifies social responsibility as one of the three main aspects of the relationship between IT and social work, along with management of services and social work practice itself (1989a). He specifically insists on the duty of social work to recognise and publicise the potential effects and disadvantages of IT. He fears, though, that the profession is in danger of lagging behind and may miss its last opportunity to shape the new technology: "The need to influence the development of information technology in line with social work needs and values has never been more urgent than it is today" (Cnaan, 1989a: 9-10).

He persuasively argues double jeopardy through social work's laggardness in coming to terms with IT: firstly, by not using the technology to provide a more effective service it is doing a disservice to its clientele. Secondly – and in the long run of quite fundamental societal importance – by not being involved in the crucial debate on the social control and social uses of new technology, it is denying a voice to the disadvantaged sector of society to whose interests social work is dedicated to serve. And if social work is not there speaking up for the dispossessed, then who will be? This issue is revisited in a later paper where the necessity for agencies to invest heavily in IT for the sake of the clients is explored: "More agencies without access to information technology means decreased resources, which may further accentuate the gap between the haves and the have-nots, both among agencies and among practitioners" (Cwikel and Cnaan, 1991: 116).

Ideological Issues

There are different ideologies and approaches to the introduction of IT. Some of these are antithetical to computerisation or indeed to other forms of "modernisation" or "rationalisation", while others view the introduction of IT as a worthwhile goal in its own right. Cnaan's reference to "the science of muddling through" is an apt exemplification of the first approach. He says: "As Lindblom noted, as long as we can 'muddle through'; doing what we did yesterday and making minor adjustments here and there; successfully using intuition, experience, rule of thumb, experts' opinions and messages from our environment, why invest in planning and data processing?" (Cnaan, 1988a: 4). This is written in the context of computer illiteracy generally, but is of particular relevance to social work management.

At the other extreme, the vigorously committed approach to computerisation can be exemplified by Brinckmann: "So my first conclusion will be: wherever and whenever a human service is structured in a bureaucratic way ... service workers will find on the market a good supply of useful information technology applications ... It follows, and this is my second conclusion, that in other fields *service work has to be restructured and adapted to the requirements of the hard- and software offered on the market*" (Brinckmann, 1989: 22, emphasis added). In this instance, instead of the customer it is the computer which is always right! This hard-nosed approach, dominated by an ideology of mechanistic managerial efficiency instead of professional integrity leaves no room for any notion of social work values or ideology at all (Phillips, 1990). Karger and Kreuger take up the cudgels against Brinckmann's world view. They accept that computers increase efficiency with reference to repetitive tasks but warn us that effectiveness is a more elusive goal in the social services (1988: 120).

Other proponents of IT are not so thoroughly mechanistic as is Brinckmann. Vallee (1986) poses a choice within a highly computerised environment of "Digital Society" versus "Grapevine Society". This mirrors LaMendola's vision of "end user" computing (1986) and the demand by Murphy et al. (1987) for "reflexive computerisation". Cnaan claims a lack of compatibility between the values of social work and those of IT: "It is our contention that the social work culture and the computer culture are for various reasons either seemingly or actually incompatible" (1989a: 7) He goes on to set up a picture of computer culture as being individualistic and idiosyncratic, rarely requiring coordination or cooperation. This association of idiosyncrasy with the world of computing rather than with the world of social work is unusual – computer culture is more often represented as being mechanistic. He concludes with the following: "Coming from such an alien background it is not surprising that many social workers are antagonistic to the new information technology, that many have had some negative experiences with computers, and that some are quite simply cyberphobic". Hammer and Hile (1985) refer to work in the mental health field which leads to similar conclusions. They identify one source of resistance to computerisation lying in value judgements about the appropriate role for computers in human affairs. They cite Weizenbaum's argument that the important question "is not whether computerised treatment applications can be made to work, but rather whether they *should* be used, even if they are shown to be effective" (Hammer and Hile, 1985: 7).

We have some good news for Cnaan and others who bemoan the seemingly unbridgeable gulf between the cultures of social work and new technology. In Chapter 3 the relationship between the two cultures will be explored and it will be seen that they have more in common than is apparent at first sight.

Professional and Organisational Issues

One fundamental factor, which cannot be ignored, is that there is a lack of congruence between the primary objectives and orientations of social service managers and social work practitioners. The social work profession is dedicated to providing a flexible individualised service based upon the acknowledgement of the uniqueness of each individual's needs, whereas social service agencies and their managers must be concerned with value for money, territorial justice, and equity both between and within client groups (Sainsbury, 1977). This leads to differences of expectations of IT between the two groups. Caputo (1988) summarises the differences thus: "The professional worker in a human service organisation serves two masters each at odds with the other: her professional self, with those intellectual and moral criteria, and her employing organisation, with its demands and constraints". From the professional perspective the client was the prime beneficiary of the services, while for administrators priority lies with protecting the interests of the public at large, and particularly the taxpayer. This critical tension "places bureaucrats and professionals at odds" (p. 61).

Forrest and Williams report that managers want aggregate statistical information for planning, monitoring and evaluation; financial information; and personnel information. Practitioners on the other hand want client information; resource information; practice-oriented procedural information; and professional practice development information (1987: 10-12). It is possible that practitioners overestimate the extent of their likely use of IT once it is in operation, but this does not make them any more sympathetic to the views of managers (van Hove, 1989: 13). Williams and Forrest note that the extent to which advances in computing bring benefits to social service practitioners depends largely on the way in which IT is developed in the future. Benefits for practitioners will only accrue if systems are deliberately exploited as a tool for professional as well as managerial uses.

Superimposed upon this lack of congruence between the two major interest groups is the straightforward fact of life within hierarchical organisations of the drive for managerial efficiency and the pursuit of cost-cutting. Thus the introduction of New Technology is often used to implement new and more efficient management practices. In their introduction to a collection of papers on Technology and Human Service Delivery, Murphy and Pardeck (1988: 2) make the point that organisations can become increasingly "rationalised" following computerisation, thus standardising practitioner-client interactions. They claim that interpersonal sensitivity is sacrificed to increase efficiency. Van Hove (1989), under the heading "Worthwhile automation involved thorough reorganisation" gives a good example of this phenomenon:

> A first level of a more active approach is reached when measures are introduced to secure consistency within the agency ... A second level is reached when changes are proposed which improve the efficiency of the organisation. We established a clear typology of the help measures the agency sees as its tools, and the conditions which rule their applicability. This allows social workers to propose help to their clients in a less haphazard way. ... We simplified the procedures ... by cutting away a lot of dead wood ... We were thus able to adjust the workloads of social workers on the basis of more objective criteria. A third level of active intervention was reached when we started rethinking the tool set of the agency itself, with the objective in mind of promoting independence of clients and doing away with all traces of paternalistic meddling both by individual social workers and by the agency as a whole (van Hove, 1989: 14).

The use of terms such as "consistency", "efficiency" and "objective criteria" (not to mention "dead wood" and "paternalistic meddling") gives an indication of the gulf which sometimes exists between managers and practitioners, a gulf which encompasses conceptions of the nature of social work itself as well as more immediate managerial issues.

Leaving aside for a moment the distinctive nature of social work as a profession, Murphy and Pardeck underline one of the facts of life of IT: that computers change all organisations into which they are introduced. "Computers create a unique presence in an organisation, which requires that life be altered in many significant ways. Some of these changes are merely logistical, while others are conceptual" (1990a: 1). Hammer and Hile (1985) reiterate this point and stress that taking possible changes into consideration at the planning stage can make the difference between success and failure. Cnaan agrees and stresses the threat of disruption to the power balance and working relationships within an organisation from the introduction of new technology. He believes this is particularly true for social work compared with other professions given that social work at present has a high level of discretion. He sees this being put at risk and on these grounds concludes that "resistance to the new technologies on the part of social work practitioners is both justified and appropriate" (1989: 5-6). These comments are rather unguarded. Concern is certainly justified and appropriate whereas resistance, arguably, should be held in reserve until practitioners are able to judge the motivations and actions of management more clearly.

Issues which are less controversial, but still provide ample scope for increased friction, relate to the implications of the administrative implementation of new systems. Job descriptions have to be rewritten and social workers will find the daily processes of their work changing. Handled sensitively this may not be a problem, indeed it may lead to positive outcomes. Cnaan, however, takes a pessimistic view: "In terms of social work practice, this job redesign will require more reporting, data collection, broader professional exposure, a lower level of individual recording, and more detailed explanations of professional activities – tasks that most social workers dislike and will do their best to avoid" (Cnaan, 1989a: 6). This doom-laden prophesy has come true in some instances, but fortunately not in others.

One of the major themes underpinning this book is the argument that this debate on organisational issues is misconceived. Many commentators and researchers assess and evaluate IT in social services agencies on management terms rather than using social service standards. Our thesis is that IT can be integrated into a social services setting within the value framework of the social services themselves. Therefore IT in social services agencies should be evaluated within a social services frame of reference. This does not mean that its implementation will be unproblematic or that there are no value conflicts within the organisational setting of a social services agency. But the crucial factor is that the starting point for both the analysis and the implementation should not be within the realms of IT theory or management theory, or even within narrowly defined social work theory, but within social services as an organism as well as an organisation.

Conceptual Issues

A problem central to the future of social work theory as well as to computerisation concerns the possibility or otherwise of codifying the knowledge-base of social work. Van Hove takes a strong line on the lack of a clear paradigmatic approach to social work: "Uniqueness of the client-social worker relationship is often claimed, we believe, to mask the confusion and lack of precision in the language of social work. This state of confusion lets social workers muddle on without a sense of direction; goals are not clearly defined, and an evaluation of effectiveness becomes impossible" (van Hove, 1989: 13). De Graaf, in more measured tones, concludes his insightful review of social work computerisation in Holland with a query of universal significance: "This brings me to a question that I cannot answer just now. Is it possible to define the main terms used in social services in a logical and unambiguous way? There have been a lot of efforts to do this in the past and they have all failed" (de Graaf, 1987: 18).

This debate is taken up further by Gripton, Licker and de Groot in an article which discusses a personal consulting decision support system developed by the authors. They take an uncompromising stance: they insist that social workers will have to change their ways if new technology is to be effectively introduced. They demand changes in the collection and use of clinical data and the quality of output measures – "measures of actual practice effectiveness". They also identify a major mismatch between the logic of decision support systems, which is linear "whereas popular theories of family therapy are based upon cybernetic models" (1988: 85). This total mismatch in the structure and process of reasoning appears to be a fundamental barrier to the use of the present generation of decision support systems in modelling the more complex and holistic aspects of social work decision-making.

This difference in ways of thinking is mirrored by differences in ways of conceptualising social work. Linear (or even polynomial) causal models have their basis in the logic of positivism and they facilitate (or even require) comparison of like with like. A positivistic logic base, mono-causality, simplicity of measurement and ease of comparison all lend themselves to an equity-based management-oriented system, which is epitomised by the decision support system. What Gripton et al. characterise as a cybernetic model, arguably it is more appropriate to call it a humanistic model, is based upon utterly different premises; those of interactive and multiple causality.

Cnaan, in reviewing the literature on expert systems, compares the problems of computerising decision-making in social work with that in even the most systematic and rule-bound of disciplines. For example he cites the case of physics where it took seven years to assist in ultracentrifugation runs and then makes the point that in social work knowledge engineering is more difficult because: "knowledge in social work consists of many exceptions to numerous, incongruent rules; competing approaches which co-exist; and personal insight and tact: all of which are foreign to the systematic logic of computers" (Cnaan, 1989a: 4). Hammer and Hile (1985) talk about a difference in "cognitive style" between the worlds of computers and social work, and they tell us that some commentators refer to the field of mental health social work as being essentially "pre-technological".

Even if these seemingly insurmountable problems do eventually get cracked and meaningful expert systems are developed, they will not give a complete answer. Murphy and Pardeck (1988) warn us about the dangers of relying too heavily on fixed rules and over-formalisation in social work, but this danger seems to be wide of the mark in relation to expert systems at least. We will take an example from one of the "hardest" social sciences where fixed rules abound – econometrics. McNown investigated the characteristics of the seven most important banking forecasting models and found that human judgement accounts for over a fifth of the variance in all of them (and nearly a third in three of them). In even this highly formalised and mathematical science human judgement plays an important part on three counts. First, the values of many important variables have to be estimated rather than precisely measured: second, adjustments have to be made for persistent errors; and third, "If forecast is unreasonable; subjective adjustments are made to the equation and/or variables until a reasonable forecast emerges" (McNown, 1986: 368).

Therefore, even in the precise, mathematical and esoteric world of econometric modelling the notion of a "fixed rule" in the total information-decision process is only tenuous. In the messier, imprecise, down-to-earth world of social work, bedevilled by the vagaries of the free choice of wayward individual human beings, the fixed rule becomes even more problematic. We will see in Chapter 7 when we explore the practicalities of expert systems in social work that "fixed rule" quickly gets transformed into a tentative "rule of thumb".

Without the security and certainty of fixed rules the introduction of IT into social work decision-making via either decision support systems or expert systems must be undertaken circumspectly and with humility. Major factors which need to be addressed include: the characteristics of "clinical" data (i.e. measuring the problems and difficulties of service users); social work measurement data (effectiveness); and overall strategies for the delivery of social services in relation to the knowledge base (or knowledge bases) of social work. In this context it is crucial to evaluate our use of IT by its application in a social service setting. This is not a structural question but one of flexibility of application.

Intraprofessional Issues

Pardeck illustrates the issues involved in using a technology that is quantitative in nature by posing the question of whether "the discursive, non-quantitative interventions which now dominate social work practice will have to give way to therapies based on a strong scientific orientation, such as behaviour modification, cognitive restructuring or task-centred treatment" (1990: 57).

Following on from this we have a conflict within the social work profession between "scientific" social work (specifically behavioural and "research based" modes of practice) and humanistic approaches. It is interesting to note, for example, the difference of approach between Murphy and Pardeck (1988) and Holbrook (1988). For a forceful exposition of "scientific" social work see also Glastonbury (1985). Behavioural and allied approaches to social work are more amenable to computerisation than the others and it seems likely that there would be less resistance to IT in social work agencies from proponents of these approaches.

Custom and Practice

Ideological, organisational, professional and intra-professional issues all coalesce around one practical focus; the everyday custom and practice of the working environment. Here the professional and organisational justifications for inertia reinforce each other. Resistance to change can virtually always be defended in the short term because of the diswelfares associated with reorganisations, but this defence is markedly strengthened by recourse to disruption of professional judgements. And these arguments are fortified by the sheer power of inertia itself – "if it's not broken then don't mend it" has a strong appeal. These arguments too, are not explicitly predicated on self-interest, they are (or at least can be claimed to be) based on altruism. The thrust of the argument is that the organisation itself will suffer from these changes.

It is clear that many advocates of change have been thwarted by the unwillingness of front line workers to countenance change in their daily routines and practices. Gripton, Licker and de Groot, commenting on an attempt to introduce a decision support system in a social work agency make the following exasperated comment: "It appears that human service professionals' habitual ways of processing clinical data are very difficult to alter. It is not easy to design user-relevant and user-friendly software for clinical practitioners and then persuade the counsellors to use it" (1988: 78). It is easy to sympathise with this but at the same time it is conceivable that the authors may have alienated the workers by making unreasonable, or at least impolitic, demands upon them (as we saw in the previous section) to make radical changes in their working practices. Gripton et al. have much to learn from Monnickendam and Yaniv (1989) who demonstrated that computerised systems can be designed to fit in with, rather than disrupt social work custom and practice.

Thus we must be careful in investigating custom and practice. There is a difference between resistance to change in daily procedural activities and resistance to change in the essential nature of social work itself, under the pretence of making procedural changes. The former can be overcome with tact and democratic decision-making, whereas the latter is an entirely valid resistance which should be supported.

Closely related to custom and practice issues are fears about possible status devaluation or even loss of jobs in social work. Butterfield takes us down a path which starts with the sensible and all-too-real worry that computerised testing, diagnosis and treatment have real dangers of encouraging lazy practice, continues through a vista of client self-help and ends with the possibility of devalued social work and even redundant social workers. He begins by discussing the growth in use and increasing sophistication of computerised tests which can be scored more quickly and accurately than previously. The fundamental danger in this, he tells us, is that testing becomes "too easy" and lazy professionals or even untrained persons are able to use tests which should be used only by highly trained and sensitive clinicians. This, of course, could all end in self-diagnosis and treatment so professionals face loss of jobs.

His next port of call concerns diagnosis. He cites work by Greist et al. which seems to show that computers can do a better job of predicting suicide risk than professionals. He comments: "Some writers are concerned that, even if *such programs are shown to be effective, they will not produce socially appropriate diagnoses for people make judgements based on non-rational issues*" (Butterfield, 1986: 13). He seems to be saying that an effective diagnosis by a computer of e.g. predicting suicide risk (to use his example) may be less socially appropriate than one made by a human clinician on the basis of non-rational criteria which, by implication at least, is less effective. Under these circumstances perhaps it would be best for all concerned if this clinician were to be made redundant at the earliest opportunity. Behind all this muddle and blatant special pleading there is a real danger which must be confronted – but it must be confronted with clear thinking.

Gender Issues

Very little has yet been written on gender issues relating to social work computerisation. Cnaan has raised the question as to whether there are personal issues which go beyond those of different conceptions of social work and even of social work values. He argues that the limited use of new information technologies may, in part, stem from the characteristics of social workers and their clients, namely that the majority of them are female. He claims that, in general, women are less technically oriented and less interested in computers than men and adds: "Whether the issue is one of different cultural perspective ... or one of unequal opportunities ... it remains that women are less inclined to work with new technologies" (Cnaan, 1989a: 5).

No specific evidence is made for this claim, either in employment in general, where it is extremely likely that the majority of workers who use computers are women, not men, or in social welfare agencies, where the majority of people who work on computers are certainly women (unless there are agencies unknown to the authors which employ more male than female clerical and secretarial staff), or indeed within the profession of social work itself. And is it really true that it is women who are most vociferously opposed to (or even "less inclined to work with") new technologies? If there is evidence on this specific claim than let us see it.

Reisman (1990) provides a far more balanced approach. She explored societal patterns of gender inequality in computer use in four major areas: the leisure industry; the media; education; and the family. She concluded that males are involved in more conducive interactions with computers than females and receive far more support from societal structures in using new technology. She insists that social work educators should recognise that these patterns occur and that they are well entrenched within the social fabric. This approach is supported by the work of Eastman (1991) who, in addition to exploring some conceptual and historical issues, provides information, advice and a resource list for women's groups.

Hyperbole and Unreal Expectations

These problems are generally worse than might be expected. Even amongst people who by no stretch of the imagination could be called enthusiasts there is often a deeply held belief that computers can work miracles. When they find out that computers do not always solve problems, disillusionment can set in. The scars of many early attempts to create client information systems in British social services departments were still being felt 10 years later (see Montgomery, 1986, for a perceptive account of the history of client information systems in British social work). Van Hove has also made some pertinent observations on what he calls the "myth" of computer efficiency: "Computers are often introduced in situations of confusion and disarray in the belief that the mere introduction of this high technology will resolve those difficulties. Furthermore, the faith in these machines is so large that one tends to forget that the people who have to make them work are more important than mere computer power" (van Hove, 1989: 13). Computer salespeople, of course, in general do nothing to disabuse agencies of these myths – at least before making a sale.

Lingham and Law who have been involved in most of the large-scale developments in UK social work computerisation, remind us that the losers from these sorts of inflated expectations are the very people social work is supposed to help. They point out that, although IT provides tools to support and improve recording and communication practices, it cannot, all by itself, change basically inadequate operational and administrative performance: "Thus any expectation on the part of social services managers that a "quantum leap" may result from purchasing some off-the-peg software and a collection of new personal computers, amounts to a dangerous delusion to promulgate with staff and an uncaring deception for the clients who happen to be the subject of the records" (1989: 124).

Bronson, Pelz and Trzcinski, in their guide to computerising social services agencies, warn about the two different ends of the hype spectrum. They refer to the pessimistic end as "Pandora's box" reactions: fears that the computer will dehumanise the agency, disrupt relationships with clients, or eliminate their jobs. At the other extreme there are "magic box" reactions, where staff believe the computer will easily solve problems with the manual information systems and will instantly produce error-free bills and reports: "'Pandora's box' reactions can produce resistance and anger, 'magic box' reactions can produce false expectations that crumble into frustration and disillusionment. Don't get boxed into either extreme!" (1988: 18).

Personal Efficiency Hype

Many claims have been made about computers changing people's professional lives by making them more efficient. For example Carlton "Perk" Clark, an independent social work practitioner, summarises the benefits for him of using computers under the following heads:

1) *Multiple Use of Information*: He cites here the benefits of word-processed case notes, which can be used in several different settings, for example in a court report. This is eminently plausible and sensible. It would be hard for any but a confirmed technology hater to disagree.
2) *Synergy*: He claims that decision-making is enhanced by building upon previous work and using data stored over a period of time. He cites resource usage and financial planning as important areas here. His examples, though, are not too convincing: "For example, an agency supervisor has at his or her immediate call, the financial data covering any specific facet of the organisation for every year that these records have been entered. Amassing this data in accessible form empowers the supervisor to make rapid, informed decisions" (Clark, 1988: 17).
3) *Extending "reach"*: This is similarly unclear: "A large task is to communicate with clients and colleagues. When the process that forms the written outreach is strengthened, eased and empowered, one's reach is also lengthened. Hence, I now write more letters, proposals, presentations and papers. Block to my professional expression has been removed" (ibid.). If he is addressing himself to the advantages of word processing and electronic mail over pen and ink and the postal services then he has a point, but if he is trying to say more than that then his case is unproven.
4) *Accessing existing research*: There is no doubt that, used properly, computers can do this, but Clark's claims in relation to his own practice are overdone: "For

example, I gather a more detailed process note on clients nowadays and can easily search the material for underlying trends and hypothetical ideas that propel my thinking and practice in very tangible ways". Now, it is certainly true that one can use the "search" facility in a word processor programme to find a specific word or phrase, and it is equally true that programmes are available for undertaking qualitative content analysis research, but Clark is here making claims on the basis of hope rather than experience.

To give him due credit he does mention later in the article that "gathering information can become a hindrance, an inappropriate end in itself". Also, at the end of the article he stresses clear-headedness in purchasing a computer. But the important issue is that he starts off by rightly identifying the proven benefits of word processing but then extrapolates on a grand scale on the basis of unproven expectations.

The "Paperless Office"

One of the recurring fantasies about computerisation is that it will eventually obviate the need for paper. Lohmann and Wolvovski, writing in 1979 made this prediction: "A ... major consideration which is currently possible in even the most basic of information systems would be to circumvent a major portion of the tremendous volume of paper consumed in conveying information. It is conceivable, for example, that in the near future, a complete agency word processing system might be financed out of saved expense for paper, duplication and copying" (p. 415). Over a decade later we are still waiting with bated breath!

Other Issues

Lingham and Law (1989) who were involved in pioneering one of the first major client databases in the UK gave a disheartened rendition of a series of interrelated technical and practical problems in moving forward with IT. They bemoan the absence of any national strategy on the part of UK local and central government or of the social work profession to encourage standardisation in operational practices, terminology, definitions and methods of recording. They also berate the IT industry's inability or unwillingness to introduce greater operating compatibility. The UK is certainly not unique in this lack of government, professional or industry attempts to co-ordinate, consolidate or standardise. Fortunately there is now some movement on this problem and it is possible that by the turn of the century these irritating and debilitating incompatibilities will disappear.

Technology Transfer

Several commentators have pointed out that technology transfer from commercial settings which took place because it was cheaper than in-service innovation, has over-emphasised hierarchical, managerial and efficiency-oriented applications

rather than therapeutic, professional development or client-empowering innovations. Along with the technology that is transferred from the business world, their
alien culture is transferred too. LaMendola (1986) warns that social work will have
to imbue its IT with its own culture in order to avoid being swamped. This echoes
the warnings of Murphy and Pardeck (1988), amongst others. Such an endeavour
is not easy. If past experience is anything to go by, both social workers and IT
specialists will have to work hard at communicating with each other in order to
succeed in developing an effective computer system which is consonant with the
culture of social work (Levitan, 1985; Garrett, 1986; van Hove, 1989).

An example of a problem in technology transfer in practice-based programmes
was encountered when educational programmes designed for use in infant schools
were initially used in social education centres for adults with learning difficulties.
Some of these service users felt patronised by the child-orientation of the programmes and did not wish to continue using them. The problem was only overcome when the new adult-focused programmes were developed (Phillips, 1986b).

Small Markets

This problem is seriously exacerbated by the smallness of the total market for social
work software. Markets for management software tend to be strictly national
because of the different definitions of what constitutes social work from country
to country and because of widely differing legal requirements. Glastonbury (1990)
is cautiously optimistic. He believes that in Britain at least the political impetus
exists to be more sensitive to market potential, although this carries dangers of
competition rather than co-operation in developments. For the present, though, he
is less sanguine: "much British software is not easy to locate, is still harder to access,
and is generally not made openly available" (1990: 2). Finnegan, Ivanoff and Smyth
(1991) mirror Glastonbury's anxieties about the dangers of competition. They
believe the entrepreneurial model is problematic specifically because of the problems of market limitations. They fear that the profit motive may drive social work
software developers to make the programme as general as possible. The resulting
lack of specificity would then decrease the likelihood of it being useful to the
individual practitioner.

The effect of small markets on the life of an IT programme can be seen from
the following Israeli experience. As a result of the growing use of computers at
local government level a private software company designed a programme for local
social service departments which included both administrative and service provision data systems. It was initially purchased by three social service departments
and the software company expected that other social service departments would
buy the programme if it proved successful.

In fact, it did work well but other social service departments were reluctant to
purchase it because it was not supported by central government social service

administrators. Those key actors preferred a predominantly administrative budget-control programme than the more service-oriented approach which the company provided in this programme (Eaglstein and Berman, 1993). The software company could not afford to provide regular updates for only three social service departments so the programme soon became outdated and unusable.

The problem for practice-based programmes is even worse. There have been many innovative and imaginative programmes developed for direct practice with clients, but these tend to have been produced on a voluntary basis, without the professional graphics and backup available from commercial products. Also, these tend to be low down on the list of agency priorities for resource allocation (Phillips, 1986b). This perspective is supported by Cnaan. He notes that word processing, spreadsheets, statistics, graphics and databases are the most commonly used packages in agencies and says "It is not surprising then that most social work academicians involved in the new technologies found that computer use in social work was limited almost exclusively to administration (Cnaan, 1989a: 4).

Reinoehl, Brown and Iroff are more optimistic. Using a user-friendly and graphically oriented computer they were able to customise off-the-shelf software for computer-assisted life review of clients. They comment "It is the belief of the authors that there currently exists a broad range of relatively inexpensive, commonly available computer programmes that, although not originally designed for human services, can become quite useful when applied in a creative manner" (1990: 49). The development of highly user-friendly hypertext media and authoring systems should lead to more innovations here. It is interesting to note that there has been an extensive cottage industry of home-grown practice-based software developed by enthusiastic social workers and their associates (Phillips, 1985a, 1986a, 1989). While such a diversity of developments creates logistical problems, it at least indicates a considerable groundswell of support for relevant IT for social work practitioners.

Cost

One truism which often gets forgotten is that capital expenditure incurs current costs; and the maintenance of computer systems can be very expensive (van Hove, 1989). Put another way: hardware and software do not work without "human ware", which is very expensive (de Graaf, 1987). Finally Garrett (1986) perhaps cynically asserts that, far from saving money, computers actually lead inexorably to increases in expenditure.

The Response of Service Users

Perhaps surprisingly, this is an area where few problems have emerged. In surveys of the literature by Butterfield (1986) and Mutschler (1986) the general response was that service-users were as happy, if not happier, communicating with computers than with human practitioners. Mutschler comments: "most clients find the interviewing process enjoyable. In fact several studies have suggested that as subject matter becomes more sensitive, such as counselling for drug problems or sexual dysfunction, respondents appreciate the computer interview even more" (1986: 50). In the welfare benefits field the findings are even more unequivocal. Joyce Epstein, after analysing the results of 398 interviews with users, reported that the overwhelming majority enjoyed their session with the computer. "People found it easy, enjoyable and productive. They were able to use the computer unaided and they coped with it, making entries, understanding the instructions, and answering the questions. People were highly enthusiastic, almost euphoric, immediately following use" (Phillips, 1986b: ii).

Dawson, Buckland and Gilbert (1987) stated that the four main advantages of a welfare benefit advice system identified by the public were: (i) a more impersonal service in answering sensitive questions on income and house composition; (ii) local access to advice; (iii) accurate and comprehensive benefit information; (iv) provision of procedural advice which assists them in dealing with social security personnel. The potential for a computer to depersonalise the process of claiming benefits was viewed as a wholly positive outcome.

Nurius and Hudson (1989) give a positive appraisal too. They were surprised at how honest and uninhibited clients tended to be in their responses, particularly regarding sensitive or controversial topics. On the basis of six empirical studies they claim that clients are often more self-disclosing and less embarrassed about revealing personal information to a computer. More dramatically, they tell us that a significant percentage actually prefer computer-assisted assessment to conventional methods, including face-to-face interviews. Unfortunately, they do not tell us just how big this significant percentage is.

Conclusions

Looking back over the reasons for underdevelopment there are grounds for optimism. Practitioner resistance, organisation and management, and research and development have produced stumbling blocks which can be overcome. The nature of social work itself is an issue to which we return in Chapter 3, but for the moment all we need to say is that some types of social work intervention are more amenable to computerisation than others.

Thinking to the future, there is much work to be done yet on the philosophical issues, particularly in relation to value systems, but these are abstract questions of great generality. They are important in the long run but need not hold us up. Ideological issues, too, are less of a problem at a practical level than they appear to be when viewed from the lofty heights of theoretical discourse. Ethical issues, on the other hand, can immediately lead to serious practical problems, but these can be resolved if IT is implemented within a social work value framework. Social work professionals and system developers need to work hand-in-hand to resolve technical difficulties over security of data. More importantly, though, social workers have to maintain their ethical vigilance over confidentiality and the best interests of their clients.

Conceptual issues do pose problems, as do intraprofessional issues, and we need to proceed with humility on both these fronts. Professional and organisational issues are genuinely thorny too, and they will not go away. But they are the stuff of office politics and power the world over, so we need not be too frightened of them. The issues of custom and practice, and those which follow, all need to be dealt with transparently but are soluble.

Overall the future can be faced with cautious hope – but only if our central message is taken on board – that it is social work values which have to predominate over IT values if computerisation is to be successful in the social services.

CHAPTER 2

People and Computers in Social Work Agencies

Much has been written about the mechanics of computerisation in the social services. There have been debates about systems theory, cybernetics and techno-rationality as well as mountains of material about the technicalities of hardware and software. But this is a classic case of starting from the wrong place. In order to understand computerisation in the social services it is essential to start at the human end and discuss people and how they – or rather *we* – respond to and interact with this New Technology.

One of the most disconcerting things about IT is that people seem immediately to view it with the same passion as sports fans – they are either for it or against it, and there can be several different reasons for being against it. Similarly, IT supporters split into different clans, and often support their own machine or their own favourite brand of software with a fervour and single-mindedness which transcends logic and rationality. So we will start off by exploring what commentators have said about these different sets of protagonists. Then we will look at some empirical studies of people's responses to IT in social work settings, trying to identify the factors which separate out the successes from the failures. This leads us finally to a classification of computerisation within social service organisations.

Personal Responses to Computerisation

Several different classifications or stereotypes of personal responses to new technology have appeared. They include: general overviews and approaches; emotional responses ranging from fanaticism to phobia; political responses, from radical managerialism to Luddite; and at a more down-to-earth level, different ways of accommodating to IT.

General Approaches

Perhaps the most straightforward general approach is the dichotomy put forward by Wilson (1989). On the one hand, he tells us, there are those with negative attitudes to using technology who are fearful about future developments, and on the other hand, those with positive perceptions of IT's impact – in other words, *pessimists* and *optimists*.

The pessimists believe technology will dehumanise and mechanise social services and will rob clients of their privacy. Wilson also claims pessimists have a fear of what he calls "peonaging"; harnessing vulnerable disabled workers in isolating technological cottage industries. As the optimists will instantly tell us, this is, of course, a two-edged sword; for many vulnerable disabled people the advent of IT provides a long sought-after opportunity for economic self-sufficiency and an improved quality of life. Optimists believe IT will allow clients to have more control over their own support system and thus gain independence and self-esteem. They also predict that computers will undertake boring and repetitive tasks more efficiently (record-keeping, for example) thus freeing up professional time for more personal contact and support for clients. Some optimists have boundless enthusiasm for IT, believing it can solve a wide range of intractable social problems. We shall meet these people again below, in the guise of *computer fanatics*.

There is another group who share some concerns with the pessimists. These are *militant libertarians*, who have a genuine and deep-seated concern over the potential implications of IT for civil liberties (Phillips, 1990). They fear, with some justification, that computerisation of sensitive data, particularly by central or local government agencies, may lead us closer to a police state. Very often they are forward-looking in their concern about the possible future implications of IT applications which at present do not seem to have adverse potential.

Finally there is a group which sits on the fence – *skeptics*. They are neither overly optimistic nor wildly pessimistic. Skeptics do not wish to implement large-scale social change without having a clear idea of the likely consequences. Similarly they tend to be unconvinced about many of the claims made for IT.

Emotional Responses

Moving away from general approaches to the relationship between IT and society and on to emotional responses towards the technology we encounter a range of responses from fanaticism at one extreme to phobia at the other.

Fanatics, or *enthusiasts* (Phillips, 1990) are totally dedicated to the new technology. Their goal is to computerise everything and anything which can be computerised, irrespective of whether it makes sense to do so or not. Many are harmless because they spend most of their time in front of a computer screen writing programmes. But they can be counterproductive in that their activities discourage any interest in computerisation among people who might otherwise be interested.

A much more intractable problem is that a disproportionate number of them seem to get into positions of power within social services agencies. The resulting attempts at introducing IT are often chaotic. Marsh, Omerod and Roberts (1986: 1), on the basis of their own experience, say "the worst possible combination is a social worker turned computer buff". This advice is echoed by de Graaf who tells us that "computer freaks do not make good advisers" (1987: 17).

Even the normally most level-headed of commentators can sometimes get carried away, and the results can be disconcerting, particularly when the enthusiast becomes exasperated by the reluctance of others to share their vision. For example, LaMendola, writing about the unwillingness of social workers to embrace IT, came up with the following commentary:

> The mainstream social worker in the United States had disempowered herself once more. She had become a member of another minority. She was a third world stereotype, technologically dependent, empoverished of tools for local development, unable to communicate in shared languages, her practice tools confined to more primitive times (1986: 2).

The defining characteristic of phobics, on the other hand, is a fear of computers or anything to do with them. This fear may extend to other manifestations of technology. Computer phobics may take great pains to avoid talking to answering machines or touching the family video. Alternatively the phobia may be more related to the numeric, mathematical theoretical foundations of computing.

To confound matters the majority of social work practitioners have very limited understanding of computer technology and have received little, if any, training on the subject, either in their agencies or on their accreditation courses (Pardeck, Umfress and Murphy, 1987; Murphy and Pardeck, 1988). Also, most social workers are reported to be cynical and fatalistic about the introduction of computerised client information systems within their agencies (Montgomery, 1986). So it would come as no surprise if a substantial body of practitioners fall into the category of social workers who "loathe everything connected with statistics, figures and technology" (de Graaf, 1987: 15).

Lamb, in her review of reasons for resistance to computerisation, explores the relationship between computer phobia and what she calls "math anxiety": "The reality of math anxiety among social work students is generally accepted ... One would assume this same likelihood is true for other human service workers". She points out that a higher proportion of females than males enter social service professions, and she maintains that the relationship between gender and performance in mathematics is strong: "In the hundreds of studies that have examined poor math performance of women ... women tend to have more negative attitudes towards math and suffer more from math anxiety than do men". Additionally, irrespective of gender, students who choose social work "tend to have a higher proportion of persons who would choose to avoid math-specific careers, such as engineering or science" (1990: 34).

In between the world of the fanatic and the phobic lies the territory inhabited by those with mild enthusiasm, neutrality or mild anxiety in their emotional responses to IT. But before investigating these relatively calm waters we have more stormy seas to explore: that of political responses to IT within organisations.

Political Responses

IT is not immune to the tensions which exist between management and workers, indeed it is a sensitive subject at the best of times. Even low levels of IT implementation such as word processing and office management systems can have far-reaching implications for job satisfaction and even job security. In times of recession and of large-scale institutional change in society, with concomitant organisational change within the social services, the age-old divide between managers and workers can emerge with a vengeance (Phillips, 1990; Karger and Kreuger, 1988). The two extremes here are *radical managers* and *Luddites*.

IT can be an excuse for as well as a cause of political tension within an organisation. For *radical managers*, determined to drag their agencies into the last decade of the twentieth century, the introduction of IT is a godsend. This band of fearless entrepreneurial change-agents will let nothing stand in the way of root-and-branch reorganisation. For them, IT is both the perfect rationale for, and the perfect instrument of, change.

At the other extreme we have *Luddites*. These workers do not just oppose IT, they will fight to the end against any form of organisational change which involves amendments to working practices. Brauns and Kramer warn us about these: "Unless one is willing to accept a purely "Luddite" approach to the application of IT as a legitimate social work strategy, it is difficult to imagine successful preventive or prophylactic strategies that are not informed by at least a rudimentary grasp of the technologies involved and an ability to assess future trends" (1987: 133).

Karger and Kreuger (1988) give a wider classification of workers' political responses to the introduction of IT within the organisational context. What we have called Luddite, they classify as *nihilist*. The aim of nihilists is to demolish the working environment by "sabotage of software or hardware (planting programme bugs), oversights in the set-up or alignment of equipment, and failure to follow rules for insuring redundancy of data storage". There are plenty of other possible avenues for nihilists. Coffee spilled on keyboards, or using diskettes as place-mats for coffee cups are effective, if amateur, nihilistic activities. But the real professionals spread viruses in the machines. Over the past decade computer viruses have become a major problem.

Karger and Kreuger also identify a less virulent form of opposition than nihilism: *rebellion*. Rebels are militantly anti-computer too but they tend to exhibit milder non-accepting responses: "On the covert side, rebellion may be used by workers increasing their use of sick days, "blue Mondays", or other subtle forms of pas-sive-aggressive behavior" (1988: 121). Next, they introduce us to an insipid form of negative reaction, which they label as "accommodation" but which might be better called "passive resignation".

Then they point to a more direct, collective political response to the introduc-tion of IT. This is described initially as a specific response to computerisation, but then takes on a much grander vision: "Constructive change can result from em-ployee demands for greater self-management, collective negotiation (in its mature form, collective bargaining) regarding the scope and intensity of office automa-tion, and ongoing technical training, in addition to the formation of white-collar unions" (1988: 122). This is a rather speedy progression from the micro intra-organisational level to the macro arena of industrial relations, and it reads like a caricature of the sort of class-warfare model of social work management which was prevalent in the heady radical days of the 1960s. It need not detain us any more here.

Their final category (which can act as a prelude to our next section, where it properly belongs) they entitle "learning survival skills". This is a much more positive response than the others they identify. They claim that this approach

> encompasses learning new technoskills, identifying new technological trends, and assessing and responding to technostress ... Anticipating the direction of office automation involves moving early to acquire appropriate technical skills, thereby enabling workers to secure a position at the workplace that guarantees them some control over new technology. And finally, office humour allows interpersonal relationships to be maintained, even though computers tend to fragment the work process (Karger and Kreuger, 1988: 122).

Apart from the adversarial framework with which this was formulated (and from the coining of that awful word "technostress") they describe a positive and sen-sible approach to be taken by anyone who is going to have to learn to live with the new technology, whether their predisposition is amicable or hostile towards it.

Accommodating to Information Technology

And it is to the area of learning to live with the technology that we now turn. Kreuger and Stretch (1990) perform a valuable service by reminding us that managers as well as practitioners may have difficulties in accommodating the new technology. They produce an elegant taxonomy of the ways social service managers can adjust to computerisation. They introduce us first to the *automation expert*, who has mastered the new technology and routinely uses it. Next comes the *mid-level adjuster*, who has made a concerted effort to understand some applications, is conversant with management computing issues and responsive to new developments. Mid-level adjusters regularly use a couple of software programmes. They can hold their own in discussions with experts and can make a wide range of management decisions with minimal dependence on outsiders.

There is a big gap between the mid-level adjuster and their next category: the *novice*. Managers who are computer novices are just beginning to become competent. They are familiar with basic terminology and applications, but are dependent upon computer experts and thus delegate a great deal of responsibility for routine administration using computer applications. Finally, there is the *uninitiated and uninterested* manager who delegates everything connected with computers. In some agencies the uninitiated manager in fact successfully blocks any form of computerisation at all.

More has been written about the response of practitioners than of managers to technology (Kreuger and Stretch, 1990; Karger and Kreuger, 1988; Wilson, 1989; and Phillips, 1990). Kreuger and Stretch provide a classification based on the notion of adjustment: *power user adjustment; moderated adjustment; ambivalent adjustment;* and *alienated adjustment.* Their first category comprises enthusiastic workers who already use a lot of software and need no training. But these power users, however, are perilously close to the fanatics we met above: "Typically they want to computerize most routine tasks. These persons run the risk of seeming to overdue (*sic*) both their personal commitment to and personal involvement in these decisions. They may be stereotyped by fellow professionals, because of what their colleagues perceive to be the constant use of jargon" (1990: 101).

The moderated adjustment group is perhaps best suited to working in an environment where new technology is being introduced. They will have learned one or two programmes and can use them with confidence. They can communicate fairly well about IT and need a moderate amount of training to achieve their full potential.

Kreuger and Stretch classify a further group as displaying ambivalent adjustment. This is a potentially confusing title because "ambivalent" is a heavily loaded word. "Anxious adjustment" is possibly a better label for this group, which has only a minor interest and very little knowledge of computing. They will require guidance and support from others. Kreuger and Stretch are a little dismissive of the potential of this group "These ambivalent adjusters thus require maximum training to become minimally functional" (1990: 102). This is a counsel of despair. Sympathetically treated, this group could easily become converted to enthusiastic and competent users of computers. Perhaps they will never become power users, but that is not necessarily a bad thing.

Their final category, alienated adjustment, comprises no hopers. It mirrors a category used by Cnaan (1989a) – that of "laggards": "The laggards are those who are the most reluctant and the last to adopt a new technology. These are generally very conservative individuals who not only dislike but are often antagonistic to change. When the laggards finally do decide to try something new, they often find that it has already been superseded by a more recent change which the innovators have already accepted" (Cnaan, 1989a: 3). Laggards are singled out for special mention for obvious reasons: "Regrettably, social work, as compared with most other disciplines, is among the laggards since it has made little effort to adopt the new information technology for use in its practice" (ibid.).

Kreuger and Stretch show a similar lack of enthusiasm about this group which is least well adjusted to computerisation: "Those who are alienated find computer applications to be a source of irritation and take pleasure when computer systems break down" (1990: 102). They claim that this group requires massive training and a lot of management support. Alternatively, they wonder if it is possibly better to ignore them totally and make sure they are not forced to become involved in computer applications.

Agency Responses to Computerisation

Agencies too have a wide range of responses to IT: from tokenism to integration and innovation. The simplest approach to IT is to ignore it altogether:

Non-Existent

Here we have the Neanderthal approach to organisational change. The agency will have a telephone and a typewriter (possibly even electric) and may well have a photocopier, but there will be no fax, no answerphone, no word processor, and definitely no computer.

Surprisingly, this sort of agency is fertile ground for introducing effective IT because it has not previously been contaminated by inappropriate or disastrous attempts at computerisation. Handled with sensitivity, patience, tact and imagination, but above all, with adequate training and orientation resources, the implementation of computers should be unproblematic and ought to pay dividends quickly in terms of quality and effectiveness of service delivery.

Low Level of Computerisation

Tokenism

Here the agency has the same negative attitude to computerisation but is more PR-conscious. Its computers are expensive, but unused, status symbols. It is highly likely that an agency which has got itself into this position is somewhat disillusioned or cynical over IT. If the introduction of the machines had been hyped up and if workers' expectations had been heightened then the arrival of the hardware, almost certainly without the necessary training backup, will have led to frustration and disappointment. If this process has not gone too far – that is, if people gave up on the machines quickly and reverted to manual procedures which actually worked – then the damage may be minimal. But if new systems dragged on for a period of time before being aborted then scars may still be painful and it could be an uphill struggle to desocialise workers from their painful early experiences. Even worse, if the system has not yet been abandoned but is "up and limping" instead of up and running then there may not be much hope unless drastic steps are taken to remotivate staff and increase their morale.

Marginalisation

Here any IT application is left to individual initiative. It is totally unco-ordinated, but at least an institutional environment exists which is not anti-computerisation. It certainly isn't pro-computerisation either, but the libertarian organisational environment (which needs to be coupled with the facility to resource computers) at least provides a setting within which IT can thrive if the personal chemistry is right.

Intermediate

This is the level where the majority of agencies are at present.

Compartmentalisation

Computers are seen in these agencies as tools for administrators, policy-makers and managers in isolation from the organisation as a whole. IT innovation takes place only within discrete areas of the agency (e.g. payroll). Within a compartmentalised agency it is possible for extensive use of computers to take place, but they will not be utilised effectively and it is possible (or even likely) that considerable inefficiencies will arise at the interface between systems. Empire-building based around control of information is a phenomenon often associated with the compartmentalised agency. Whether this is caused by or is an effect of the style of computerisation is an interesting question, the answer of which probably differs from agency to agency.

Routinisation

Here the agency responds rationally (if unimaginatively) to the IT age by using computers to substitute for manual or mechanical tasks (e.g. word processing, elementary file management). The routinised agency is not dissimilar to the compartmentalised agency except that the advent of IT is planned on an agency-wide basis, or at least on a systematic basis. Here we arrive at one of the crucial elements for the success of effective introduction of IT – holistic, systematised planning. In this case it is not dramatically exciting or imaginative, but nonetheless a quantum leap has been taken. The possibility now exists within the agency of e.g. report writing, where the authors input into the same document from different physical and organisational locations, incorporating narrative and spreadsheet material and possibly also head-counts from computer-indexed case files.

Once this starts to take place on a regular basis then the agency is on the threshold of a high level of IT implementation.

High

Here the qualitative change which commenced in the routinised agency takes root and grows. The organisation becomes information-rich and communication-friendly. This state of affairs has great potential for positive (and also, regrettably, for negative) outcomes.

Integration

The organisation itself changes because of the integrative effects of a holistic approach to IT within (parts of) the agency, for example, integrated office systems and client information systems (Sircar, Schkade and Schoech, 1983). These changes will have far-reaching consequences within the organisation. A dynamic source of power and energy becomes unleashed. The central theme of this book is concerned with exploring the issues surrounding this very situation.

Innovation

The very highest level of IT in a social work organisation is when the introduction takes place of completely new innovations possible only with IT.

This level is the epitome of the synthesis between the worlds of social services and of IT, when the social services use IT to carry out tasks which they would be unable to carry out otherwise. This means that they are not merely using IT to do an existing job more efficiently, faster or differently, but rather implementing a process impossible to carry out at all in a practical manner without the use of IT as a part of that process.

As will be seen in Chapter 5 a whole new branch of social work practice, "case management", is developing in the USA and UK in response to new government policies in community care, and its success is to a large extent dependent upon IT for its needs assessment, resource allocation and service delivery effectiveness.

Other innovative implementations range from the exotic to the mundane. At one extreme are the apparently far-fetched and futuristic possibilities of clients using "smart cards" for therapy or monitoring or even financial aid. At a more prosaic but nevertheless revolutionary level there is the prospect of interactively matching client needs with practitioner interests and expertise at the client's referral or first contact with the agency, leading to immediate and appropriate case allocation. This could possibly be followed by "distance therapy" through a combination of communication devices and IT resources – for example, linking CD-ROM, video discs and expert systems and putting their resources at the disposal of practitioner and client (using operating systems of course which enable expensive hardware to have multi-user remote site access).

Social Work Computerisation in Practice

Armed with some idea of the range of possibilities of computer applications in the social services, let us now look at what developments have actually taken place. We start with an overview covering a large number of agencies and then look at a couple of detailed case-studies.

Empirical Quantitative Studies

There is only a limited literature on staff attitudes to the new technology and on levels of computerisation in agencies, but fortunately the few recent studies have all been large-scale. We have found a total of six studies between the mid-1980s and 1992: three of individual social workers (402 in total) in areas in Canada, the USA and Israel and three of agencies (covering 331 social service organisations, all in the USA).

Workers

One of the three studies has a large sample but provides limited information, while the other two go into considerable depth but have relatively small numbers of respondents.

Senner, Young, Gunn and Schwartz (1988) report the responses of 296 social workers and psychologists in Saskatchewan and South Dakota in 1985. Altogether, 22% of the social workers had a home computer and 35% used a computer at work (with a slightly higher use in Saskatchewan than South Dakota). The social work uses of computers were, in order of magnitude: administrative database management; financial analysis and accounting; word processing; research and data analysis; and education (the authors provide no further breakdown or even percentages).

Pardeck, Umfress and Murphy (1990) obtained detailed responses from 59 licensed certified social workers in a mid-southern state of the USA in 1986. Over three-quarters had access to computers in their agencies, but less than half of these used them in their practice, and even fewer on a daily basis. Over a third never used a computer at all. Only 7% had an educational experience which prepared them for using the technology, but 35% did have some in-service training. Around two-thirds felt that computer technology should be included in social work education and a similar figure said that in-service training should be available. Wagner's study of agencies, discussed below, has similar findings. He reports problems in training staff to use the machines. Some agencies which had students on place-ments from courses where IT was taught reported they were using the students as *de facto* training consultants.

Pardeck et al. studied both usage and attitudes of staff towards computers. The highest usage was for storage and retrieval of records, followed by programme evaluation and other kinds of research. In only about a fifth of the agencies which had computers were they used by social workers for letter writing or other word processing, and in an eighth of cases for writing computerised case records.

With regard to attitude, almost two-thirds agreed or strongly agreed that computers can improve their effectiveness; but only 7% assented to the question "Can computers actually do therapy?". A total of 84% agreed with "Does a computer help a social worker to manage information effectively?". Nearly half thought computers were a threat to client confidentiality but over a half thought computers assist practitioners in assessing a client's problems. Over three-quarters thought computers increased organisational efficiency and a half thought computers enable practitioners to assist an increased number of clients. Less than a fifth thought that the dignity of clients was jeopardised by computers. Less than a quarter thought computers would drastically change the nature of social work. All in all, this seems to be a highly positive response. They conclude: "The attitudes of social workers towards computers were somewhat unexpected. In particular, they had very positive attitudes as to the assets of computer technology. However, strong doubts were noted concerning computer use in therapy and questions were raised in the area of confidentiality. These doubts appear consistent with the humanistic base of professional social work" (Pardeck et al., 1990: 126).

Monnickendam and Eaglstein (1992 and 1993) undertook a very detailed statistical analysis (predominantly using factor analysis) in a study of the attitudes of 47 social workers in Israel. They explored three factors which are mentioned in the literature as relevant: intrinsic attitudes of professional personnel towards computer utilisation; organisational factors (such as support, commitment, planning, involvement and resource allocation); and finally, system design factors (including ease of operation and mastery of the machine, impact on treatment process and organisation of work, extent of routine use and accessibility). Their main aim, however, was to attempt to determine factors which affect computer acceptance and use.

They conducted a literature review which identified many recommendations for successful implementation of the computerisation process, but could find virtually no research findings in social work to support any of the recommendations.

Although their study was small and their findings must be treated with some caution, they came up with two interesting conclusions. First, for their sample at least: "Computer phobia is a non-issue. This is unexpected and good news". Secondly, they provided a list of factors related to satisfaction with implementation: (i) ease and satisfaction during routine implementation; (ii) intrinsic belief in the ability of the agency to implement the computerisation process; (iii) worker involvement; (iv) feeling that the process was well planned (Monnickendam and Eaglstein, 1993: 422). Their final conclusion was that "Social Workers do not believe the computer to infringe on the worker-client relationship and do not fear for the dehumanisation and depersonalisation of clients" (Monnickendam and Eaglstein, 1992: 10).

Agencies

The most astonishing thing about computer use in agencies, particularly micro-computers, is its recency. In the earliest of the studies, undertaken in the early 1980s, less than half of the agencies had computers. In 1986, the majority of agencies had computers, but most of them had computerised only in the previous two years. Wagner comments: "It appears that the use of microcomputers in social services agencies is a relatively recent phenomenon, even in the heart of 'Silicon Valley', made possible by the development of systems that can handle larger programs, the advent of effective mass storage via hard disks, and by the rapidly declining prices of efficient computer systems" (1987: 82).

Finn's 1988 study incorporates a brief literature review and reports on a survey of 160 private agencies in North Carolina in an unspecified year in the mid-1980s. Hooyman, Nurius and Nicoll (1990) report on a study of 103 agencies in Seattle undertaken in 1986. Wagner (1987) canvassed 100 public and private agencies in Santa Clara county in "Silicon Valley", California in 1986. He received 68 replies.

Hooyman et al. (1990) found that four-fifths of agencies used computers for word processing and over half used databases, spreadsheets and/or financial tracking programmes (in descending order). Wagner (1987) reported similar results. The pattern was similar, but at a lower level of implementation, in Finn's study. This difference may be explained by an earlier research date or possibly the private agencies which he studied were later developers than public agencies. The latter explanation is supported by the data from Hooyman et al. They found that the private agencies in their sample had consistently lower computer use over the range of applications than did public agencies.

Managers and administrators made more use of the computers than did the professionals. Hooyman et al. found that three-quarters of agencies used comput-ers for administrative tasks. Finn reported that computers were used by direct service workers in only a third of agencies. Hooyman et al. had more positive results on direct service tasks, but again this can be explained by higher usage in their public sector sample. Overall, 60% of the agencies reported using a computer to perform one or more direct service tasks. These included: case tracking; client intake; information and referral; assessment; and recording.

They found that large agencies were more likely to be computerised than small agencies. They also discovered that practitioners were using the machines more often than they had expected: "In addition, direct service workers were heavily represented among social work users of computers, even in administration-based tasks" (Hooyman et al., 1990).

Case-Studies

We have looked at studies of computerisation from the perspective of the agency and the workers separately. It is not easy, though, to bring these together to get an overview by using statistical sample surveys. So we now turn our attention to comparative case-studies. There has been a large number of one-off case-studies of computerisation, some of them in very great detail (for a classic example see du Feu, 1982) but only very few recent comparative studies. We deal here with two major studies, one of eight agencies in Canada which were already computerised and the other of the differing fortunes of two agencies in Israel which were embarking upon the computerisation process.

An In-Depth Study of Eight Agencies in Canada

Gandy and Tepperman (1990) report on a long-term in-depth study of a sample of eight agencies, chosen to represent both "people-changing" and "people-processing" agencies of different sizes. They were highly critical of most previous publications dealing with perceptions, attitudes, successes and failures in social work computerisation because they claimed they were normative and prescriptive rather than being grounded upon rigorous empirical investigation.

They used a two-stage sampling approach. First they canvassed 253 social work agencies within an 80 kilometre radius of Toronto. They got replies from 172, of which almost a half (82) used computers. Large organisations used computers more than small organisations and more than half were newcomers to computers, only having introduced them within the past two years. They found that five activities accounted for most of the computer use: accounts and expenditure; report writing; word processing; planning or policy making; and analysing client characteristics. These findings are consistent with those of the three agency studies noted above. They then selected eight of these agencies to study in depth.

Their book is crammed with details of the effects of computerisation in the eight agencies but there is a paucity of broad conclusions which can be generalised to other agencies. Partly this is due to the in-depth qualitative approach they adopted which was highly empirical. They say of their regular meetings with their research workers: "There was much marvelling at any discovered pattern or similarity between organizations. What the field staff found was simply so distant from what the literature had led us to expect that we were constantly confused, constantly at a loss" (Gandy and Tepperman, 1990: 32). They criticise other writers who had generalised across agencies but perhaps they became so engrossed in the details of the agencies they studied that they were unable to see the wood for the trees.

Their overall finding was that the impact of computerisation was much less marked than expected. In particular, the majority of direct service staff felt it had little effect on supervisory arrangements. On the other hand, a majority of managers (60%) and a substantial proportion of supervisors (40%) felt it had a positive effect on supervision. The researchers' conclusion was that computerisation did give managers more control over their staff and therefore, indirectly, over clients. This is because of their increased potential to continuously monitor worker performance.

We have more to say on the implications of their findings in Chapter 4, but for the moment it is worth remembering that the predictions of both sides in the normative debate seem not to have been met. First, the computers do not seem to have had much impact on the organisations, and secondly the staff using them do not feel strongly inconvenienced or oppressed by them. Gandy and Tepperman also say:

> Our findings are also inconclusive about the effects of computerisation on social control over clients and staff; this is another area where further research is needed. We saw no evidence that computerisation had changed control patterns in significant ways, though in one or two organisations control may have tightened somewhat. But what we saw was far from the drastic fears of totalitarian management hinted at in the social welfare literature (Gandy and Tepperman, 1990: 184).

Implementation: Two Case-Studies in Israel

Mutschler and Cnaan (1985) explored two large-scale implementations at national level, one of which succeeded and the other one failed. Several factors seemed to be crucial.

First, the unsuccessful agency initiated a top-down implementation with very little consultation. No line workers or supervisors were included in the planning committee. For example, the commitment of key individuals, such as the managers of each welfare office, was only sought after the objectives of the system, the forms to be used, and the timetable for implementation had been designed. Even then, they were asked to cooperate but not to provide input or feedback. Consequently the system was oriented towards serving the decisions and goals of administrators on the national level rather than to provide information to line workers and managers in the local offices. On the other hand the successful agency involved all branch managers and a selection of line workers in each phase of system development and implementation. Their suggestions greatly influenced the subsequent design of input and output forms produced by the information system.

The actual design of the forms in the unsuccessful agency led to a great deal of extra work for line workers. They often had to make home visits to the clients for no other reason but to complete forms which would be of no use to them. This resentment led to Luddite responses; many forms were incomplete or fabricated.

The system's objectives and uses of data were not related to workers' day-to-day tasks and merely led to additional gratuitous paper-work. In contrast, the successful agency's information system facilitated the decision-making of line workers as well as administrators and branch managers. Consequently, representatives of all three groups participated in the development of the conceptual design. For example, line workers' suggestions led to the inclusion of additional service and outcome categories which administrators would not have considered important. Input forms and data management procedures were discussed and revised repeatedly and were only used after they were approved by administrators, branch managers and line workers on the committee. The administration's willingness to spend the necessary time and resources on involving and educating staff members and to produce easy-to-use input forms paid off with a more trouble-free implementation and less resistance to change. The vital factor here was that although there were costs involved to the workers – completion of the computer forms was more time consuming than filing in the old handwritten notes – these were outweighed by the benefits which had been built in via the extensive consultation process.

The unsuccessful agency also botched the system testing. Training sessions were held during which staff were instructed on filling out the forms. But not enough resources were allocated to data processing. As a result, the incoming forms could not be coded and were piled up in corridors and on the floor of the computer office. As we saw from Monnickendam and Eaglstein (1993) success at this stage is a crucial factor in staff confidence. The final ignominy was that the completed system provided the decision-makers with no useful information to help them to improve the quality of their work, plan services more effectively, or assess outcomes of the services provided.

It is obvious then, that there is a right way and a wrong way to implement IT in a social services agency. The whole of Chapter 6 is devoted to this issue.

Conclusions

A cursory glance at the wide range of possible individual and agency responses to computerisation might give rise to concern. Imagine the consequences of a combination of fanatical managers and Luddite social workers. Indeed, such a combination did come together from time to time in the early days of mainframe computers. Fortunately, this catastrophic scenario is now not common because there is greater understanding on both sides of the possibilities and limitations of IT in social work agencies. If care is taken then conflict between managers and workers can be avoided. Nonetheless, there are serious conceptual issues in the relationship between social work and IT, as we shall now see.

Part II

CONCEPTUAL, ORGANISATIONAL AND POLICY ISSUES

CHAPTER 3

IT and Social Work: Conceptual Issues

In Part One we explored a range of general issues surrounding the utilisation of IT within social work. We now turn to the heart of the issue and investigate the specifics of the relationship between social work and IT.

Social Work and IT

It quickly becomes apparent that social work has many theoretical strands, some complementing each other, some in conflict, and each facet has different implications for IT. But IT too, does not have a singular and fixed identity in relation to social work practice. So there are a myriad of possible ways of bringing IT and the social services together. We explore this intersection and take a pragmatic approach towards finding common ground.

Conceptions of IT

Within the social work profession there is a lack of clarity about the nature, purpose and possible impact of IT. Steyaert reminds us that social workers, by and large, have traditionally seen IT as a threat to their professional status and humanistic values. Faced with the challenge of IT many turned their backs and ignored it. Unfortunately for them, IT did not go away, it was implemented without their involvement: "Because social workers never really took up the challenge, the present introduction of IT applications does not follow social work rationality but the rationality of system analysts. Therefore the present introductions are a threat to social work and social work values. This is clearly a vicious circle" (Steyaert, 1992: 20). It has to be said, of course, that the rationality of systems analysts is the rationality of IT.

But what exactly is IT? So far in this book we have discussed the subject at length but have not yet provided a formal definition. LaMendola (1987) bites on the bullet and makes one of the rare attempts in the social service literature to define "information technology". He does not find it an easy task. He beats about the bush for a couple of pages before coming up with the following: "It would possibly be most accurate to define information technology as the codification of the human way of doing things with data in order to derive meaning" (p. 55). In using this formulation he is bending over backwards to find a definition which is as user-friendly as possible to the social services, but in doing so seems to obfuscate rather than clarify. His motives are noble: he is trying to make the important point that IT did not commence with computers. For example, the use of video in social services education is well established and acceptable. He is on the right track because he is trying to find a way to conceptualise IT in a way which is relevant to the social services and can be taken on board within the context of its value system.

It is important at this stage to make a distinction. There is a difference between what IT *does* and what IT *is*, between its utility and its structure. If we concentrate our attention on structural technicalities, on what IT actually "is", then we are likely to get bogged down either in metaphysical assertion and speculation or to become overwhelmed by technical details. On the other hand, if we concentrate on utility, and ask what it is that IT can do for us then we will get a clearer and more useful idea of its possibilities.

An extreme example of metaphysical assertion is given by Wilson: "Technology *demands* characteristic ways of thinking ... Technology *sets its own objectives*, and would have us evaluate progress towards those objectives in terms of its own criteria and logic (Wilson, 1989: 49, emphasis added). Fortunately, this sort of approach is rare, even in social services literature. But there are many less blatant examples of the notion that IT has an active identity, that it is in some sense *alive*. This notion leads to IT taking a central place in the organisational framework and with the technology itself, instead of the purposes for which it was introduced, playing a dominant role in organisational activities. A classic example of this is Murphy and Pardeck's (1990a) contention that computer technology participates actively in shaping its own environment and that "techno-rationality" necessarily dictates the structure of working environments in organisations. This overly-deterministic and rigid formulation implies that IT will necessarily permeate every aspect of the organisation and will significantly affect its structure, value system and personnel. In this perception of the nature of IT the social services organisation ends up with the tail wagging the dog. It changes its activities for the sole purpose of fitting in with the technology instead of doing what it should be doing and using the technology to enhance its activities.

Kling (1980) criticises this approach to the nature of IT: "Only the most ardent technical determinist would claim that the consequences of computer use depend exclusively on the technical characteristics of the mode of computing adopted" (p. 62). Yet when we look at the literature on IT in social service organisations we often find such a deterministic approach (Boguslaw, 1981; Brinckmann, 1988; Kraut, Dumais and Koch, 1989; Meyer, 1986; Wodarski, 1988).

An alternative perspective of IT based upon its utility is to view IT as *a technological means in achieving organisational or professional goals*. In this approach IT possesses no intrinsic value in itself but rather attains value by being used purposefully. This may be called a utility-centred approach to IT. Isaksson (1991) writes "Computerization reinforces the prevailing structure – this means that an undemocratic system becomes more undemocratic with computerized routines and a democratic system becomes – or has the necessary requirements for becoming – more democratic" (p. 3). Kling states that "computing is selectively exploited as one strategy among many for organizing work and information. The patterns of computer use appear to fit the workplace politics of the computer-using organization" (1980: 78). The utility-centred conceptualisation of IT places it firmly within the everyday control of organisational decision-makers. Kling's findings indicate that the technology does not necessarily lead to a dramatic change in the character of work; indeed it can have a benign and even totally inconspicuous influence on the work of the computer user. He characterises the role of IT as being determined by the needs, norms and values of the organisation. He goes on to say that computer-based information systems reinforce the structure of power in an organisation. "Automated information systems should be viewed as social resources that are absorbed into ongoing organizational games but do not materially influence the structure of the game being played". He then concludes "computers by themselves 'do' nothing to anybody. Computer use is purposive and varies between social settings; little causal power can be attributed to computers themselves" (Kling, 1980: 100). This is in stark contrast to Wilson's doomsday scenario, reported above.

How should we then conceptualise IT? It is obvious from the differing perspectives above that its nature, or its *identity,* is socially constructed. If, as we would wish, it is seen in terms of the uses to which it can be put then obviously it can do good or it can do harm. And there are at least two ways in which harm can be done – deliberately or through miscalculation (or, in political science terminology, conspiracy or cock-up). If, on the other hand, it is seen as an all-powerful technological persona which actively determines aspects of organisational environment then it may do good or harm but it will certainly constrain the activities of individuals within the organisation.

Or perhaps it is social work which can have an identity problem? Social work's humanistic, socially sensitive, participatory, interactive value system ought to prevent IT from becoming the dominant factor in the organisational framework of the social services agency. At the same time there is a danger of lack of knowledge, fear, distrust and a general negative bias to IT which might prevent social workers from developing an appropriate perspective which would enable IT to have a positive impact within the social services. Therefore, the social construction that is given to IT within a social work agency is related to the perspectives of social workers. And these, of course, are influenced by conceptions of social work itself.

Conceptions of Social Work

Social Work has a complex nature. There is much common ground on its purpose and even, at least on a high level of abstraction, on its value base. But it has a diversity of theoretical paradigms, problem-solving strategies, and perspectives on interactions between service user and social worker. This can been seen either as a healthy diversity or as hopeless fragmentation – or a mixture of the two.

Things were not always this complex. Social work has gone through a series of stages during its development and growth, each of which has left its mark. The initial impetus in the nineteenth century was motivated largely by philanthropic concern about the high levels of human distress that were identified by empirical social investigation. At the turn of the century, with the introduction of social work within university educational settings, came the beginnings of a move away from the profession's charitable and individualistic roots and of a trend towards social work as an "applied social science". Then in the 1920s the (in)famous "psycho-analytical deluge" commenced. This was followed by the development of the insight-oriented diagnostic school which was heavily influenced by Freud. His theoretical work gave social work the credentials necessary for it to gain scientific stature.

Subsequently a wide range of new theories and approaches blossomed in the era of rapidly expanding welfare provision after the end of the Second World War. The functionalist school (which had been around before the war) was joined by a range of theories drawing on the disciplines of psychology and sociology, which themselves were expanding rapidly, and thus spawned even more social work theories. At least four main strands had developed by that time, each based on a different tradition: empiricism, drawing upon natural science; "insight" based on deep self-knowledge; the "scientific psychology" of learning theories and behaviourism; and sociological theories of symbolic interaction and structural inequality. The natural science paradigm was pretty straightforward and homogeneous, but each of the others spawned a range of differing theories (Howe, 1987).

It is not surprising, therefore, that attempts were made to consolidate and attempt to unify social theory (and, along with it, the social work profession) via the unitary "system theories" of the 1970s. System theory of course led to a false dawn for social work: "In spite of the widespread fashion for systems theory throughout the 1970s, the unification of social work theories was premature, incomplete and illusory. It was the product of epistemological myopia" (Howe, 1987: 21).

Running parallel with these developments within social work were larger social movements throughout the developed world. Social work was not immune to the political radicalisation of the 1960s. This challenge to the scientific approach to social work began in the United States when the War on Poverty called for outreach, grass-roots and community services. Throughout the 1980s and into the 1990s this political strand in social work has developed into a systematic critique of inequalities and the development of anti-oppressive and empowering social work practice strategies.

Social work in the 1990s is thus a complex entity encompassing a wide variety of theoretical and ideological traditions. Howe (1990) attempts to make sense of this by identifying four different paradigms, each with its own label:

- functionalists: "the fixers"
- interpretivists: "the seekers after meaning"
- radical humanists: "the raisers of consciousness"
- radical structuralists: "the revolutionaries"

These paradigms relate to two dimensions in social work theories: between order and conflict; and between subjective and objective.

He sees the fixers as empiricists operating within the functionalist paradigm and having an objective view of social reality. System theories, behaviourism, task-centred approaches and even psychodynamic theories come within this group (or at least the psychodynamically influenced psychosocial approaches of e.g. Hollis). Loosely, we can call these approaches "scientific social work".

The seekers after meaning are best exemplified by client-centred (Rogerian) approaches, "loving" (Halmos), interactionalist and labelling approaches. Humanism, love, art, intuition, understanding, appreciation, are all used in this paradigm. This is social work as "art".

The raisers of consciousness include adherents to radical social work, client empowerment, feminist and anti-racist practice. Based in a political analysis, their aims are to raise awareness and take control. Their methods include consciousness raising, collective action and organising for power.

The revolutionaries aim for a radical redistribution of wealth and power. Their methods are those of aggressive welfare rights work and collective action via socialist and Marxist social work (unfortunately Howe does not tell us what the latter entails – and we have not been able to find any other source to enlighten us either).

These two latter paradigms have two similarities which are of interest to us. First, they both take group and community perspectives; they deal with neighbourhoods, communities or groups which share a common interest. Secondly, they are concerned about change in society.

The difficulty with Howe's classification lies in the very fuzzy border between his "fixers" and "seekers after meaning", particularly in relation to psychosocial theories. Their very nature leaves them with a foot in both camps. For heuristic purposes he is postulating a split at the art-science border where in reality the shading between them is more akin to that of a continuum. Markus makes a helpful contribution to this area:

> One of the most pervasive themes underlying social work practice and education is the confusing and complex interface between art and science in therapeutic counselling, these two approaches seem at times to blend together in near-perfect harmony and at others to lock horns in unresolvable conflict. ... The helping professions have developed and learned to live with these apparent incongruities: art is art and science is science and apparently the two are forever entangled and intertwined and never the twain shall part (Markus, 1990: 31).

Social Work and IT: The Nature of the Relationship

So, where does this leave us? If we take a utility-based perspective on IT we can define its nature for our purposes as "a technological means for achieving professional or organisational goals". The nature of social work is more problematic but we can at least identify a "mainstream" art-science continuum, along with two, more peripheral, strands of community orientation and concern over societal change as relevant features.

It is clear from Howe's list of approaches within his "fixers" and "seekers after meaning" paradigms that most of our time will be taken up with the mainstream of the art-science continuum, but the "fringes" occupied by the "consciousness raisers" and "revolutionaries" need to be touched on here. Their community and group orientation is indicative of a commonality of interest with community activists and pressure groups in general over the use of new technology (Eastman, 1991). Concern over social change (which is shared by some elements in the mainstream paradigms too) is a large issue which transcends the day-to-day problems of social workers grappling with technology in their working environment. Rather, it leads to the expansion of the social services to take on board wider issues of social justice and empowerment (Bevan, 1998). Here the relationship between IT and social work is clear. It is imperative for social workers in their wider role in social development to embrace the technology and to disseminate its benefits to the disempowered (Cnaan, 1988a).

Back within mainstream social work, at the science end of the continuum social work is seen to be dependent on a body of quantifiable knowledge, systematically derived from experience. Social workers at the art end of the continuum, while not denying the value of learning from experience, see social work practice partly as an expression of the intuitive, creative, and imaginative talents of the practitioner (Goldstein, 1990). Obviously these are stereotypes, but for purposes of analysis it is useful to categorise science and art as opposite ends of a continuum.

Where does IT fit on the continuum? Can we hypothesise that IT will be predominant in social work practice at the science end whereas artistic social work will push IT to the background or avoid it altogether? At first sight this seems an attractive proposition, but a more measured investigation will reveal a less stereotyped answer. The scientific method and technology both lead to the expectation that the social services are subject to control, measurement, prediction and systematisation. IT can be perceived as the technological application of scientific principles in the social services. The greater the scientific characteristic of a social service process the more applicable it should be to IT. Certain social work models such as behaviourism may be based on scientific concepts and therefore be more conducive to IT.

At the other end of the continuum where art dominates, IT will not be a primary consideration. Goldstein stresses the uniqueness of social work interactions: "Upon entering our clients' lives and worlds, we quickly discover that we are dealing with uniquely personal and often opaque personal constructs and stories" (1990: 38 and 41).

But even the most die-hard artistic practitioner of the social services will concede that social service work has a knowledge base of "practice wisdom" which is the accretion of knowledge, insights, skills and values. While the sources of this knowledge base and its application vary according to the different schools of thought of the profession it still forms the basis for social work.

In social work, as in any other profession, information is a key factors in the delivery of services. Information technology can be used to facilitate the creation of "working knowledge" via the process of transforming "knowing" to "doing" (Layton, 1974). Social work practice is the application of that "working knowledge". Information technology can enhance this working knowledge without adversely affecting "the honing and conscious use of the individual, the intuitive and interpersonal skills that allow real communication between persons" (Turem, 1986). Social work practice does not therefore have to be seen as the scientific application of a technological decision. Social work practice can be seen as the "artistic" application of social work values based on a working knowledge of a social work knowledge base.

The role of IT changes as the social worker moves from a scientific application of the knowledge base to an artistic application of the knowledge base. The "scientific" social service worker may translate scientific knowledge into technological knowledge thereby applying IT. On the other end of the continuum, the "artistic" social worker may completely avoid IT, but if IT is used sensitively it can play a useful role in the life of an art-based social worker. But a lot of work needs to be done before this can come to pass. The crucial task is to shift the balance from a technological paradigm to a humanistic paradigm. Just how much needs to be done can be seen from the following case-study of what can be seen as the epitome of a fusion between IT and scientific social work.

Behavioural Social Work and IT: A Case-Study

Terry Holbrook in a seminal article advocates a "marriage" between behaviour therapy and computer technology given that the principles and practices of behaviourism dovetail effectively with the programming and monitoring capabilities of computers. This leads him to predict "that behaviourism or some variant of it will be utilised increasingly and promoted as the ideal therapeutic approach to complement the computer revolution" (Holbrook, 1988: 89-90).

The basis of his claim is not just the chance coalescing of a social work paradigm and new technology. He sees both as being in the vanguard of the advance of science: "Because of behaviourism's identification with ideas, values and patterns of thought associated with modernisation, e.g., progress, faith in science, the quest for mathematical certitude, and prediction and control in decision-making, this theory will continue to shape the future for a long time to come" (ibid.).

His detailed exposition of this position is worth quoting in full:

> Computer technology has also been heralded as providing solutions to the difficulties involved in information processing, production and control. There are a great many theoretical and practical similarities between behaviourism and computerisation that lead logically to their effective combination. Computer programming, for instance, assumes that most decision-making is routine, repetitive and follows rational rules. Information processing requires that data (behavioural or otherwise) be objectified, decision-making criteria be clearly outlined (process), and service units assume a measurable form (output). Behaviour therapy, on the other hand, assumes that all the therapist has to do is target a specific behaviour, introduce a stimulus (input), and modify the stimulus until the desired behavioural change occurs (feedback). Both technologies are based on the premise that complex human behaviours can be reduced to their simplest parts, manipulated, and altered to attain some predetermined goal. Since both technologies are goal-oriented and stress measurement, as a result of establishing clearly defined objectives and specified frames for change, the capability for judging success or failure is built into each system (pp. 91-92).

These sentiments are a long way removed from the artistic end of the social work spectrum, and the proponent of artistic social work will quake at the notion of behaviourism as the ideal therapeutic approach to complement the computer revolution. Indeed Holbrook's exposition is almost a parody of "ultra-scientific" social work.

Holbrook, while accepting the closer links between behaviourism and computerisation and acknowledging that its higher level of "scientific street credibility", comes to balanced conclusions which give comfort and support to the whole range of the "art-science" continuum. He accepts that psychotherapy in general has been seriously undermined by behaviourally inclined researchers whose scientific research challenges seriously the effectiveness of "talking therapy". On the other hand he shows that conflicting evidence and arguments for both sides have appeared in the literature. He concludes that behaviourism is probably winning, not because it has necessarily been shown to be more effective, but because it is more in tune with the tenets of positivistic science. But he is by no means convinced that this will always continue to be the case: "Depending on one's definition of science and scientific evidence, there probably will always be inconclusive evidence pertaining to which therapeutic method is best" (Holbrook, 1988: 104-105).

It would provide an elegant and well balanced end to this section if a case-study of the effective use of computers in "artistic" social work were to be presented. It is possible to point to computer applications which are of benefit to artistic social work (e.g. computer conferencing and networking). Unfortunately, however, as yet there are no "artistic" examples which match the forcefulness of the behavioural case-study. One of the main reasons why scientific social work has such a lead in the application of IT is that technological values have for too long predominated over social work values in the implementation of IT. A primary cause of this lies within social work education. Its greatest sin has been of omission; IT has little or no place in most social work curricula. But even when it has been covered the teaching of IT in social work education has long been dominated by a technological paradigm. But, as we will now see, an effective humanistic IT social work education paradigm is now appearing. It is to be hoped that in the not too distant future this will lead to the development of more IT applications of specific benefit to artistic social work.

Social Work Education and Information Technology

Education is the life blood of any profession. Not only does it provide the initial period of socialisation into knowledge bases, norms, mores and values, but it also is the process through which professions revitalise themselves. Innovations in theory and practice are disseminated by researchers at the cutting edge of new developments. These university academics publish their results in the scholarly and professional press, and, more importantly for our purposes, devise curricula and teach the students who are new recruits to the professions. Social work education has a proud tradition of introducing successive generations of social workers at the beginning of their careers to the state of the art in social work.

It is particularly vital in an area such as IT, where knowledge is expanding so rapidly, for schools of social work to be at the forefront of providing an appropriate, relevant and professionally valid introduction to the possibilities of new technology for social work. Sadly, even as we write in 1994, there have been perilously few attempts to introduce IT into social work curricula. Nurius, Richey and Nicoll (1988) conclude that there is little evidence that social work educators have adequately responded, or are sufficiently prepared to provide effective training in this area. Indeed, some responses have been of little service to the development of the knowledge base, value system and professional legacy of social work.

Weick (1987) claims that it is this professional legacy which gave to social work its wisdom about the worth of individuals and the fostering of a commitment to the importance of values in the practice of social work. So, what impact does the introduction of technology into the schools of social work have upon social work's value system? In answering this question Weick found that social work educators embraced both the necessity of disseminating social work values and the importance of empirical scientific knowledge in social work education. Yet Weick concludes that the balance has shifted significantly away from values and they have become subordinated to knowledge as evidenced by the ubiquitous maxim of "knowledge-guided practice". Saleebey (1991) takes a more extreme view of the relationship between science and values in social work. He claims that many of the implicit values of technology "subvert the unique and defining values of the social work profession" (p. 51). In this battle for the minds (if not the hearts) of social workers, Dean and Fenby (1989) remind us that social work educators play a crucial role in developing student awareness of the intellectual traditions of the social work profession.

Finnegan and Ivanoff (1991) report on a study of the effects of brief computer training on the attitudes of students towards computer use in social work practice. They conclude that schools of social work do develop links between social work values and technology used in social work agencies: "The mandate to prepare students to meet the changing technological demands of professional practice is also an opportunity to prepare them to participate in shaping the face of information technology in practice to reflect social work values and knowledge" (Finnegan and Ivanoff, 1991: 81). LaMendola (1987) points out that all students entering social work must be computer literate but claims that IT courses are inappropriate unless they have particular and specific social work content.

A review of the literature leads us to the conclusion that there is a continuum between, at one end, those who concentrate upon the technical aspects and, at the other end, those who stress the centrality of social work values in the teaching of IT in schools of social work. We label these as *the Technologists* and *the Humanists*. Towards the middle there is a substantial group whom we call *the Techno-Humanists*.

The Technologists

Among those who take a technological approach to teaching IT are Cnaan (1989b), Monnickendam and Cnaan (1990), Lamb (1990), Schwab and Wilson (1990), and Reinoehl and Mueller (1990). The distinctive characteristic of the technologists is that they emphasise IT *per se* as the focal point in their education programmes. This emphasis on technology is consistent with Imre's view of the empirical model in social work, as "social work's embeddedness in the culture of its times" (Imre, 1984). The premise of the technological approach is that social work education should accommodate itself to the new technology.

Cnaan (1989b) believes that social work education should be responsive to IT developments: "Due to the number of applications and the constant changes they undergo, and the demand for computer-literate graduates, social work education should concentrate on familiarizing students with general computer applications" (p. 236). He recommends that social work students should know how to use at least one word processor, one database and a statistical, graphics or spreadsheet programme. He contends that it is unnecessary to teach programming skills and that specific, detailed knowledge can be developed at a later time when students enter employment. He believes that it is vital for IT to be incorporated into core courses rather than being sidelined into separate technical courses (pp. 237-238). Cnaan's approach focuses specifically on IT but he does see its role as being reactive rather than proactive, in that it derives from the requirements of social work agencies. Nowhere, however, in his educational framework does Cnaan address the issue of professional norms or values.

In a later paper Cnaan joined Monnickendam to present a course outline for teaching IT to social service students in order to "meet the needs of the future" (Monnickendam and Cnaan, 1990). Their course outline consists of two interrelated and integrated modules: theory and practice. The theoretical approach is largely based on system theory, decision theory and organisational theory. The practicum module is aimed at providing the student with basic tools to apply the theoretical function to concrete problems and situations. Students are introduced to the university mainframe computer and/or to personal computers. By means of a series of exercises they learn to use the operating system, to manipulate files and to carry out basic word processing. The course is assessed by a term paper comprising a proposal for the design of a computerised process in a social service agency.

Lamb (1990) similarly takes an approach which is dominated by the technology. For example, in her curriculum all social work students are required to use statistical packages. It is not surprising that she experienced "subtle faculty resistance" to the incorporation of computer technology into the curriculum. She concludes despondently that: "It will be unfortunate, indeed, if much of social work education continues to educate students in a computer void, failing to address state-of-the-art capabilities necessary to achieve optimal functioning as a professional" (p. 41). Schwab and Wilson (1990) take an even more mechanistic approach. They insist on teaching programming languages to social work students and even as late as 1988 were still requiring their social work students to learn BASIC: "It is argued that a programming language approach is essential if the social work profession is to assume responsibility for the ways in which computers are implemented in social services" (p. 77). It is fortunate that theirs is a lone voice. It is a fundamental misconception to believe that the nuts and bolts of programming languages are of any importance to social work students. It is far more important for them to gain a broad understanding of the capabilities of IT.

This was given recognition when the entire output of the journal *Computers in Human Services* in 1990 (Volumes 6 and 7) was devoted to the notion that "computer literacy" is a basic prerequisite for introducing IT in the social services. The two volumes surveyed IT in social work education as it was about to enter the last decade of the twentieth century. The guest editors were Richard Reinoehl and Thomas Hanna for Volume 6 and Richard Reinoehl and B. Jeanne Mueller for Volume 7.

Reinoehl and Hanna's definition of computer literacy in the social services is "the ability to use or develop computer applications competently within the context of human service theory or practice" (1990: 6). This is a useful starting point but, unfortunately the concept is introduced in the context of a rigid and somewhat artificial taxonomic framework which seriously limits the definition's application. Reinoehl and Mueller widen the scope of the definition. For them computer literacy is "the intersection of computer ability and professional expertise in the human services". They identify two levels of computer literacy: functional and professional. Functional computer literacy is "the basic level of ability that enables an individual to use a computer adequately in the performance of his or her occupational roles". The professional level of computer literacy includes: the ability to evaluate computer hardware in order to select and use the most appropriate system for the intended situation; and it involves creativity and the ability to add new knowledge and tools to practice or theory by applying existing software to new situations or by developing new software for social service applications. This seems reasonable and is clearly grounded in the professional values of social work theory and practice. The content of the curriculum for teaching the professional level of computer literacy, however, concentrates heavily on the technology. It includes:

1) Advantages and disadvantages of different computers and operating systems.
2) Types and variations of software application.
3) Differences between higher level programming languages, macro, and other internal programming languages.
4) Differences between centralised and decentralised processing.
5) Ways of developing software for human service application.
6) Organisational dynamics necessary for effective computer use.
7) Processes for development and enhancement of computer systems that are both effective and appropriate for stated organisational purposes (pp. 8-9).

Reinoehl and Mueller remark that: "The last two items in this list, while not pertaining specifically to the mastery of computers, are important aspects of the milieu in which human service professionals work" (1990: 9). One might wonder if social service professionals do indeed also relate to clients.

The Techno-Humanists

This middle ground between technological and humanistic approaches to teaching IT in social work education is heavily influenced by the work of Paula Nurius presented in a series of articles over a three-year period (Nurius, Hooyman and Nicoll, 1988; Nurius and Nicoll, 1989; Hooyman, Nurius and Nicoll, 1990). Its dominant characteristic is the integration of the humanistic tradition of social work education within a technological approach to teaching IT to social work students.

Nurius, Hooyman and Nicoll (1988) say that social work agencies "wish that students be informed, creative and inquisitive potential users of computers, rather than possess particular types of computer skills" (p. 195). On this basic finding they suggest the following areas of study for a course of IT:

1) Attitudes towards the use of computers in social work.
2) History and trends in computer technology: evolving trends.
3) Understanding the basics of computer technology.
4) Examples of clinical applications of computer technology, their potential and limitations.
5) Examples on non-clinical computer applications, their potential and limitations.
6) Common software and its uses in social welfare, including strengths and limitations.
7) Legal and ethical issues regarding computer use.
8) The organisational context of applied computer technology, particularly within different agency settings.
9) Implementation issues of social welfare computer applications such as systems analysis and design, feasibility analysis (pp. 195-196).

In this course description Nurius et al. explicitly relate social work values and norms to IT. The subject areas "attitudes towards the use of computers in social work" and "legal and ethical issues regarding computer use" essentially place IT within a social work value framework. What is disappointing, however, is that in the area of "implementation issues of social welfare computer applications" only technical subjects are on the agenda, such as systems analysis and design and feasibility analysis. In an approach oriented to social work values one would expect implementation issues such as the possibility of depersonalisation of relationships, rights of privacy, and preservation of individualised care to be discussed. These issues are on the social work IT agenda (Garret, 1986; Pardeck, Umfress and Murphy, 1987; Karger and Kreuger, 1988; Phillips, 1989; Murphy and Pardeck, 1990; Cwikel and Cnaan, 1991).

In a later paper Nurius and Nicoll (1989) shift their emphasis somewhat towards the social work end of the continuum. They state that: "computer literacy preparation is consistent with the fundamental goals that shape priorities in social work" (p. 66). One of these goals is acculturation, which includes fostering a set of values which inform approaches to computer usage. They give the following guidelines for curriculum development:

1) Understanding the basic language of computers.
2) Having a conceptual understanding of a computer's strength, limitations, and its present and potential applications to social work practice.
3) Operating the computer in hands-on fashion for a variety of applications and understand the output.
4) Functioning as informed participants in agency-level planning and decision-making regarding the role and use of computers in agencies.
5) Conceptualising substantive practice questions and operationalising them in terms of the computer system.
6) Anticipating and working with potential dilemmas.
7) Innovative, perhaps trouble-shooting problems on developing new applications (p. 75).

These guidelines seem to represent a change in emphasis from the approach presented in the earlier paper (Nurius, Hooyman and Nicoll, 1988) where it was the *information technology* issues and applications within a social work setting which were emphasised. In this paper Nurius and Nicoll (1989) take on the *professional social work* issues of working with IT. This approach moves them closer to the humanist approach of IT application in social work education.

The Reinoehl and Mueller volume includes an article by Hooyman, Nurius and Nicoll (1990) which takes a much bolder integrative approach than in the earlier papers. Here they insist that all students should have a basic understanding of the following elements: the changing role of computers in social services and its applications; software applications relevant to the social services; and common computer hardware and operating systems. Students are required to have some knowledge about agency-relevant applications, to have entry-level skills in using them, and to be aware of appropriate and inappropriate uses. They are also taught to evaluate ethical questions related to computerisation.

In comparing this most recent proposal to their previous ones we find that social work values and norms now have a greater impact on the curriculum. They have also added an evaluative dimension which they relate to the whole range of IT applications within social work. This is an important and significant step towards the integration of social work values and norms with IT application in the social services.

The "techno-humanist" orientation is an attempt to ensure a balanced approach within the social work education setting to the two value perspectives. Each perspective is seen as having merit and is valued for its contribution to the social work profession.

The Humanists

The humanistic orientation includes the work of LaMendola (1987), Brauns and Kramer (1987), Pardeck and Schulte (1990) Smith and Bolitho (1989), and Hernandez and Leung (1990). The characteristic of this approach is that IT is not presented as an independent entity with its own set of independent values. Instead it is integrated within a social work value framework and goal system.

A leader of the humanistic school of IT in social work education is Walter LaMendola. He claims that without effective preparation in computer literacy, social work will be left in a position of technological dependence, disempowerment, and social reactivity (LaMendola, 1987). Therefore he concludes that IT must become part of a social worker's education. His starting point is acculturation, but he differs from Nurius and Nicoll (1989) who want social workers to acculturate to IT. He insists that it must be the other way round:

> Social work students must be taught the norms and beliefs of the profession so that, as new members of the profession, they can participate in our cultural traditions. Acculturation to the social work profession includes an introduction to a value system which relates to what people in our society believe in as well as what they have a right to expect from society (LaMendola, 1987: 59).

So, according to LaMendola, social work students should not start studying IT until they are acculturated into the social work value system. Necessary areas of IT competence include:

1) *Analytic competence*: the ability to analyse new forms of computer technology in terms of the purpose, values and methods of social work values.
2) *Practice competence*: in dealing with organisational and interpersonal factors as well as the impact of IT on the lives of individual clients.
3) *Technical competence*: the ability to use, design and develop applications.

LaMendola views IT in social work education within the framework of social work values. He does not shun technical competence and even goes a number of steps further in its use than many at the technological end of the continuum but he firmly keeps it within a social work setting.

Brauns and Kramer (1987) in discussing IT and social work education express themselves in terms which are familiar to the social work practitioner. "It is important that social workers involve themselves creatively and with a sense of social responsibility in the application of IT" (p. 132). They then say that schools of social work should expand their curriculum horizons in two directions: first by offering a broad-based programme of simple computer literacy for all students; and secondly by offering specialised courses in IT applications and evaluation from the perspective of social work's goals and intentions. Brauns and Kramer have a clear humanistic perspective of IT in social work education and they emphasise that IT applications must fit into that perspective. For them IT is just a tool of social work and should not be a dominant player in social work education.

Pardeck and Schulte (1990) describe a course for senior-year undergraduate students or first-year graduate students which is unique because it does not have as a major goal the use of IT. Instead the course is built around the theme of the influence which IT may have on the social services and thus on the individuals, groups and communities which they serve. The course is explicitly critical and analytical. Students are encouraged to analyse the assumptions underpinning computerisation and are helped to develop a critical perspective on the use of computer technology in the delivery of social services. Areas discussed in depth include: exploring how a specific computer activity may have positive or negative consequences for a client; examining student values relative to the computer workplace; thinking about computers and their social role; and appraising current literature on computers and social services.

Pardeck and Schulte recognise that IT will have a significant impact on the social services. But their response to this relationship is not to turn social workers into pseudo IT specialists but rather to enable them to understand and then use IT within a social service conceptual framework. This approach does not accept IT on its own terms. Pardeck and Schulte are educating the social worker of the future to ask: "What does information technology mean to me as a social worker in a social service setting? How can I, a social worker, best use information technology to fulfil social work goals?".

Smith and Bolitho's (1989) work on the nature of information itself led them to make some recommendations for social work education. First, they demand advanced computer literacy (seemingly at or above the professional level advocated by Reinoehl and Mueller). But they add an element of social worker control: "There has to be an understanding that the control of the technology lies with humans, and that, although the technology carries with it a different perspective to problem solving, it is still an artefact of human endeavour" (p. 95). Secondly, adding a distinctively humanistic element to their proposal, they state that more attention needs to be paid to developing and teaching conceptual frameworks which examine the way information can be generated and used by social workers in meaningful professional ways. In the absence of any clear strategy for information use, the implementation of computerised information systems leads to a deluge of useless data. It is therefore essential for students to be educated about the uses and management of information *per se* in social work as well as being taught about its technology.

Hernandez and Leung (1990) literally follow in LaMendola's footsteps. They carried out their study on IT and social work education at the School of Social Work of the University of Denver, where LaMendola originally introduced his pioneering curriculum. Hernandez and Leung claim that their curriculum model is unique in that: "It is first of all a *social work* curriculum. While computer technology and software are taught as an integral part of the curriculum, they are taught as a means to an end rather than as an end unto themselves. The technology is focused upon as a tool to enhance social service practice" (p. 117). This statement epitomises the humanistic end of the technology-humanism continuum.

Empirical Verdicts

The structure of our presentation, commencing with a technological perspective and culminating with a humanistic perspective, makes clear where our sympathies lie. We, like LaMendola, believe it is vital that social work values should provide the context for an explicitly humanistic approach to IT in social work education. This belief is supported by empirical evidence from studies undertaken by Hooyman, Nurius and Nicoll (1990) and Finnegan and Ivanoff (1991).

Hooyman, Nurius and Nicoll (1990) undertook an empirical study of 103 agencies in Seattle. "Conceptual understanding" was identified by 71% of the agencies as being rather or very important, compared with 55% for computer literacy and 44% for hands-on experience. The single clearest theme emerging from the study was that social work students need to acquire a conceptual understanding of the realities and possibilities of the role of computers in the social services. The specifics of hardware and software were considered by the agencies to be relatively unimportant. Factors considered to be of major importance were: understanding of meaningful information management; the implications of computerisation for agency functioning and service provision; and organisational accountability. Agencies also stressed the ability to think ahead creatively about how computers could be used to meet present and future needs:

> An orientation towards professional level computer literacy as opposed to functional literacy was also apparent. That is, because many agencies viewed their future hardware and software resources as uncertain and their present resources as in flux, they sought more general rather than specific training. Hands-on and technical experience were reported as desirable, but viewed as more readily obtainable on-site through training. These were thus seen as less important as a prerequisite than the professional and substantive understanding upon which technical training could build. As part of this professional socialization, a constructive attitude and minimal anxiety with computers was also consistently noted (Hooyman, Nurius and Nicoll, 1990: 105).

These findings relate directly to the technological-humanistic dichotomy of IT in social work education. A purely technological approach in social work education does not appear to be the answer to using IT within a social service setting. Perhaps technology and technique need to be subordinated to caring and to the moral and ethical energies of the profession in order to achieve a greater impact on the social work process.

Conclusions

From our analysis of IT in social work education we can conclude that in spite of the "technological fix" (Saleebey, 1991) social work has not separated itself entirely from the value perspective which gave the profession its sense of mission (Weick, 1987). To use Witkin and Gottschalk's (1989) conclusions regarding social work research we can say that the strong commitment of the profession to a basic set of core values forms an important contextual dimension against which IT must be assessed. The dichotomy between technology and humanism as manifest in the teaching of IT in schools of social work can be seen to be part of a larger issue such as "who controls the profession", the empiricist-scientists or the practising professional (Karger, 1983).

Looking back at the conceptual debate on the relationship between social work and technology at the beginning of this chapter, it is clear that, at present the scientific end of the social work spectrum is much further advanced in the use of IT than the artistic end. It is to be hoped that the emerging strength of the humanist perspective in social work education on IT will lead to a redressing in this balance.

CHAPTER 4

IT and the Social Work Agency: Organisational and Management Issues

The introduction of an IT system is a major step for an organisation. Even before any computerisation takes place the structure and operation of the organisation need to be carefully scrutinised. It is necessary to have a precise understanding of how an organisation operates before being able to computerise it. A knowledge of formal structures and systems is a necessary starting point, but it is not enough. In a "people-oriented" organisation such as a social work agency the informal channels of decision-making and communication will play a vital role – and they will not be as effectively documented as the formal ones. Indeed, they may not be documented at all.

So, it is necessary to get to know an organisation inside out in order to be able to computerise it. But one of the ironies of computerisation is that this new-found knowledge of the organisation often becomes redundant very quickly. This is because IT, once it has been introduced, can have a fundamental effect on the way the organisation works. So we need a two-stage analysis: first of the way the nature of the organisation affects the introduction of IT, and second, of the way the IT, once implemented, affects the nature of the organisation.

But before looking at social work organisations in particular we will stand back and discuss a general issue which affects all organisations – power. An examination of the dynamics of power within organisations enables us to understand how innovation and change take place. Then the dynamics of computerisation itself will be explored. Just as there are differing – not to say conflicting – theories about the ways organisations operate so too there are divergent models of the dynamics of IT implementation. Then we look specifically at approaches to computerisation within social work agencies. Very different factors are seen to operate depending on the nature and purpose of the IT implementation itself and some crucial lessons are learnt about managing the implementation of innovatory IT applications in differing organisational contexts.

Organisational Type

Rational-Mechanistic or Natural Systems-Organic

First of all, why is it important to discuss the nature of organisations in order to help us in exploring IT in social work? As we saw in Part One, it is impossible to understand IT in the personal social services without understanding the motivations, hopes, fears and professional attitudes of the social worker. It is similarly unproductive to ignore either the structure or the dynamics of the agency in which the social worker works. Karger and Kreuger, in typically uninhibited fashion make the point thus: "To discuss technology without locating it within a framework that includes its political and organisational consequences is to obfuscate rather than illuminate its hazards and potential. In short, the impact of technology is dependent on the organisational context in which IT is employed" (Karger and Kreuger, 1988: 115).

Classically sociologists have identified two different types of organisation: variously characterised as rational bureaucratic (Weber, 1964) versus natural systems (Parsons, 1956); or mechanistic versus organic (Burns and Stalker, 1961); or closed versus open (Silverman, 1970). The debate about these two organisational types is mirrored in the debate in the social planning literature between rationalism and disjointed incrementalism (Booth, 1988). Partly it reflects two different sets of activities (there genuinely *are* organisations which match each of the extremes) but it also reflects two different perspectives about the social world and social action. Are humans rational calculating beings whose world is orderly and predictable or are we intuitive, sometimes impulsive creatures who have to act quickly and contingently in response to the unpredictable vicissitudes of daily life? We all know the answer – we are a mixture of these, and most organisations of humans are a mixture too. The trick in analysing organisations is to use the analysis which is appropriate to the element of the organisation we are studying; to be in the right place at the right time with the right conceptual framework.

Organisational Structure

A typical large, multifunctional social service agency is a dog's dinner in terms of its organisational structure. A major part of the organisation will be a hierarchical, bureaucratic structure along the lines expounded in Max Weber's classic study (Weber, 1964). This will deal with the day-to-day administrative tasks common to all large agencies. It may also include social security or similar payments if they are made on rule-based criteria. Other forms of resource allocation may also be under hierarchical control.

Even within formal hierarchies, though, there will exist a hidden world of informal networks and working relationships. These informal structures may work hand in hand with the formal organisation in order to help it to work better, or they may subvert it or they may even totally supplant it. Ironically the classic socio-logical study of informal networks supplanting the hierarchy by Peter Blau (1955) took place in a social welfare agency. We will see later just what mayhem can occur when attempts are made to computerise a formal system which exists in name only – this can totally thwart the informal system and leave the agency in a state of paralysis.

Juxtaposed with this formal structure (and its informal shadow) is the collegiate organisational structure which is the norm (or at least the goal) for professionals working in an organisation. For example, academics, doctors and lawyers, by the nature of their professional status, enjoy some degree of autonomy within their working environments. There is a sphere of operation which "belongs" to them. In social work, which has a more precarious hold on the status of "a profession" than some other vocations, this area of freedom is often limited. Nevertheless the ten-ure of "clinical freedom" or "professional independence" (which encompasses the social worker-client relationship and its associated peer group appraisal and non line-management supervision) is of high priority in the social work profession. It also has considerable organisational consequences. In principle at least, social workers will be held accountable to line management for many of their actions, particularly in relation to statutory obligations and resource allocation, but will be accountable only to themselves and their peers for their professional judgement.

In reality there is seldom a clear-cut distinction here. The exercise of profes-sional judgement will often involve use of scarce resources and will have to be exercised in cases where the statutory obligation resides with the head of the agency and not the named individual worker (to confuse matters, in England the agency head is responsible in child care cases whereas the named social worker is account-able in mental health cases).

Here the interface between the formal organisational structure, its informal counterpart, and the area of professional independence lies in a murky area. In general, practitioners are able to maximise their independence in situations where their line managers and other superiors are kept in the dark as much as possible about their day-to-day work with their clients. The advent of computerised man-agement information systems (MIS) which illuminate this arena can have nega-tive effects upon practitioner independence.

But it is more complicated than this; it is not merely the case of professionals working within a rational hierarchical structure. All but the most specialised social security agencies deal with a wide range of human needs in situations which demand a flexible, individualised response over and above the specifically professional interactions between social worker and client. In other words the general social services agency must have a front-end organisational structure appropriate to the provision of diverse unstandardised services. The mechanistic rational structure of the classic Weberian bureaucracy, for all its strengths, is not up to this task.

The sort of overall organisational structure which operates here is Parsons' "natural systems" model (as interpreted by Matheson, 1993) where the focus is upon the organisation as a social entity, comprised of groups and individuals in the pursuit of their own interests. There are basic conflicts of interest within the organisation between the different informal subsystems, each with different goals. Within this context, decision-making is seen to be more complex and political in nature. The natural systems approach is helpful for analysing and understanding intra-agency (and even intra-professional) stresses and conflicts over computerisation. It enables us to envisage a pluralistic system where conflicts are dealt with by concession, accommodation, avoidance, changing the rules, or even by naked bullying.

Burns and Stalker (1961) have developed this paradigm even further. They have labelled as "Organic" the sort of structure most appropriate to the more individualised and community-oriented forms of social work, and particularly to community social work and community work itself. Not surprisingly "organic" values have much in common with those of the profession of social work; humanistic, creative, responsive and outward-looking. An organic structure does not have a clearly defined hierarchy and it involves a continual redefinition of roles. Functions are co-ordinated by frequent meetings and communications are lateral and regarded as providing information and advice rather than instructions. Individuals are expected to perform their tasks in the light of their knowledge of the overall aims of the enterprise. Such an organic structure mobilises expert knowledge without too much regard for the formal place of the expert in the hierarchy. It is suitable in unstable situations in which the organisation often has to deal with relatively unpredictable new tasks and problems.

This Organic stereotype is extreme – it was specifically designed to stand at one end of the spectrum. At the other end is the Mechanistic structure, that is: "clear hierarchy of offices involving strict specialisation, vertical communication, and the implicit assumption that 'somebody at the top' is responsible for making sure that everybody's specialism is relevant to organisational goals" (Silverman, 1970: 114-115). It is evident that very few social services agencies will be totally or even mostly organic in nature, although very few will have no elements of organic organisational structure within them. Most agencies must have some mechanistic structures, and in some agencies these will dominate. Nonetheless, wherever social work as a profession exists there will always be a tendency towards organic structures, and a degree of practitioner autonomy.

Each of these organisational elements will exert their own environmental influences upon the introduction of IT, each with a downside and an upside. The upside for the mechanistic model is obvious: routinised, straightforward, rule-bound operations are a gift for the IT implementer. The downside is whether these formal systems actually exist in the real world of the organisation (as opposed to the representation of the real world in the management structure flow chart on the director's wall). For the organic organisation it looks at first sight that computerisation would be inappropriate but the ability to marshal, codify and analyse information is a boon in a rapidly changing environment where decisions have to be made swiftly. For the professional, the computer is genuinely a double-edged sword. As we saw above it can take away power through giving additional information to the professional's line manager and it can also serve to deprofessionalise by demystifying the professional task. But, from the opposite perspective, it can place more power at the professional's fingertips. For social workers, demystification can often be beneficial: first to clients, through empowerment; and secondly to the social workers themselves by reducing the pressure of an ever expanding caseload – but more of this later.

Social Work Organisations

Social work organisations lie in between strict bureaucratic hierarchies and full collegiate professional partnerships. They are "semi-professional": professional activities do take place but they are co-ordinated and controlled by supervisors or managers who may or may not themselves be professionally qualified. Ultimately, this control is by a line management function. There is tension between the professional and the managerial aspects of the organisation. Caputo identifies four further features which characterise social service organisations. First, they are either "people processing", "people changing" or "people sustaining". Moreover they are increasingly dealing with people in holistic terms, trying to get to grips with their complex, multidimensional problems. Secondly, they have what he calls "muddled missions". This means that they are confronted with multiple expectations and conflicting demands. They are in the business of controlling as well as caring:

> For example, public welfare agencies simultaneously provide for the needs of the poor, while they face the demand to reduce welfare rolls and encourage the poor to enter the labour market. Similarly, juvenile courts pursue goals of "law and order" and "social rehabilitation". To accommodate conflicting demands, human service organisations often develop ambiguous, if not contradictory, goals (Caputo, 1988: 72).

Thirdly, they are highly dependent on resources controlled by other organisations and they have to work in an inter-organisational setting. Finally, and perhaps most importantly, they lack determinate and effective technologies. The social services in general have limited and fragmentary knowledge bases. Furthermore, social work has yet to demonstrate its effectiveness. Caputo tells us that social services develop ideological systems in place of technologies to guide and justify the behaviour of staff. This leads to a great deal of staff discretion, which compounds quality control problems and makes it extremely difficult to develop explicit performance assessment criteria. These difficulties are exacerbated by the pace of change in the social and legislative environment within which they work.

For all these reasons Caputo characterises social service agencies as being more like "organised anarchies" than rational structures. This means that they "can be characterised by problematic preferences, unclear methods, and fluid participation". This leads him to ask how information is used and how decisions are made in social service organisations. The answer he gives is that in most social service organisations, the collection and use of information are basically informal and are normally not systematic, goal-directed processes. Also, he says that decision-making is far from routine or rational in the usual sense of the term. His conclusion is of fundamental importance: Technical rationality depends on agreement about ends. When ends are fixed and clear, then the decision to act becomes an instrumental problem. But when ends are confused and conflicting, there is as yet no "problem" to solve (Caputo, 1988: 87).

The Dynamics of IT and Social Service Organisational Structure

Now that we have taken stock of the organisational characteristics of social service agencies we can start to investigate the two-way interaction which takes place with the implementation of IT: how the organisational structure affects the implementation, and how the IT, once implemented, influences the structure and very character of the organisation itself. In addressing the first of these issues we will concentrate our attention on IT innovations at the strategic planning level, and in addressing the second we will concentrate on management information systems. The use of these examples is partly based on pragmatism – they are the best documented ones – but the main reason for choosing them is conceptual. Strategic planning is a less routine activity than management information so the factors affecting its implementation are likely to be more varied and sensitive to organisational factors. On the other hand, a management information system will affect a large number of people at different levels of the organisation so any organisational change as a result of its introduction could have widespread implications whereas strategic planning is in the hands of a small number of people, all at a higher management level.

Computers for Strategic Planning: Creative Individuals
in an Uncertain Environment

Matheson (1991 and 1993) reported the results of a highly innovative and important piece of empirical research designed to explore the relationship between IT innovation and organisational factors in social service agencies. His conceptual framework related to the dichotomy discussed above between a Weberian rational versus a Parsonian natural systems organisational structure. He questions whether the traditional association (at least in publications) of computerisation innovations with the rational perspective is at all appropriate given the notoriety of the social services for lack of clarity over their goals and the fact that they are not noted for their technological refinement or organisational efficiency. From an extensive review of the literature he found several factors identified as being significant to the success or otherwise of IT implementation. The research suggests that these may combine into clusters or sets of variables, some of which are relevant to the rational and others to the natural systems paradigm. The key variables associated with technological innovation in the two paradigms are as follows:

Rational Paradigm: on the assumption that successful technologies meet organisational needs, technological change is most likely to occur when there is: (1) clarity and consensus concerning organisational goals, (2) preoccupation with organisational efficiency, (3) access to pertinent information, expertise and sufficient resources

Natural Systems Paradigm: on the assumption that successful technologies meet individual or group needs, technological change is most likely to occur when there is: (1) an organisational environment of uncertainty, (2) preoccupation among competing interest groups with access to resources, (3) organisational receptiveness to change.

Matheson undertook an empirical study of 37 social welfare organisations which made some use of computers for strategic planning purposes. Results were correlated with organisational characteristics (including size and service type) and technological characteristics (including length of computerisation, number of applications, on-site expertise, and report generating capacity).

The overall findings were that large organisations, particularly "people processing" agencies such as social security offices, which had already for many years used computers for routine activities were most likely to be found in the advanced user group. The fundamental factor seemed to be size. This is all pretty unsurprising, but his results did not stop there. The design of his further analysis of these findings was innovative and insightful. He used a "cross-case design structure", comparing "exemplars" (i.e. a large organisation with extensive computer use for strategic planning and a small organisation with only limited computer use) with "anomalies" (i.e. two limited-usage large agencies and two extensive-use small agencies). The findings were analysed within the context of the rational and natural systems organisational paradigms.

The exemplar findings seemed to give strong support to the notion of a rational paradigm. Analysis based solely upon the variables associated with the rational paradigm provides a logical explanation for the differences between the agencies.

Both agencies had clear organisational goals and both associated enhanced computer use with the aim of enhancing efficiency. And, crucially the large agency had a tremendous advantage in terms of access to information, expertise, and the financial resources to carry it through (Matheson, 1993: 389).

From a natural systems perspective, however, these factors were far from adequate in explaining developments. In both agencies the impetus for innovation came from determined individuals. In the small agency it was a board member "But for the initiative and energy of the board member who (initially) volunteered to design and implement the automated information system, it might not be in place today" (Matheson, 1991: 9-10). In the large agency it was a planner, close to the senior administrator who was central "He routinely designed and developed information systems for program managers, and assisted them with subsequent data manipulation and analysis. Without him, it is unlikely that the organisation would have advanced to the present level" (ibid.).

The view from the anomalies was radically different and flatly contradicts the predictions in the literature relating to the paradigms. From the rational perspective one would expect innovation to occur in response to organisational need for efficiency in relation to goal attainment. Therefore, goal clarity is vital. However, in the "anomalies", the organisations with the clearest goals were the least advanced in using computers for strategic planning. The *most* advanced organisations had ambiguous goals, but they also showed the most concern over efficiency: "Computerisation was seen to be the only means by which they could cope with expanding program and data requirements without increasing their administrative support staff". And computerisation was not a soft option in resource terms either: "They didn't have the financial resources to purchase computers ... and so they aggressively solicited donations of equipment. In effect they compensated for their liability of size through sheer determination". So, the organisations confounded the "rational" criteria: "Factors associated with organisational innovation that derive from the rational paradigm do not account for the levels of computer use found in non-normative examples. Indeed, they contradict the patterns found" (Matheson, 1991: 11).

The natural systems paradigm stands up better:

> In summary, the environmental conditions suggested by a natural systems perspective do seem to account for the differential use of computers for strategic planning in the four non-conforming organisations. Organisational uncertainty, competition for access to resources, and internal receptiveness to change, seem to have been far more relevant to technological innovation than clarity and consensus regarding organisational goals, principles of efficiency or access to information, expertise or financial resources. The small but advanced organisations overcame their disadvantages, while the large but less advanced organisations failed to exploit their advantages, using rational criteria for the propensity to innovate (Matheson, 1991: 13).

In his study, the only evidence he found of organisational receptiveness to change was the presence of innovative individuals:

> Every organisation in this study had a computer champion – someone considered primarily responsible for the current level of computer use for strategic planning. Even in the largest organisations, one person was singled out for his or her ability to apply the technology to agency problem solving. Ironically, none of these people were computer programmers or technicians, and few of them had formal training in the use of the technology (Matheson, 1991: 14).

Perhaps Matheson should not have been too surprised that none of these innovative individuals were computer programmers or technicians. The qualities that these people seemed to have in common was an ability to have a clear perspective of the needs of the organisation as a whole along with an understanding in general of the capabilities of IT. Thus they were able to see the goals of the organisation first and then to identify how and where IT could help to meet them. IT for the computer champion was a means to an end and not an end in itself. Previous research has shown that computer experts are not necessarily the best people to instil IT into an organisation. For example, de Graaf (1987) notes that computer freaks and salesmen are not good advisers, and Gunn (1989) asks "Does the expert know best?"

Returning to his literature review, Matheson reminds us that three themes predominate in the research findings: goal clarity and consensus, resource availability, and conditions of uncertainty. Only one of the three was substantiated in his research, but it proved to be the most critical factor: conditions of *organisational uncertainty*: "Put simply, where there was little perceived need to expand computer applications for planning, it did not occur. The less advanced organisations in this study, regardless of access to human or financial resources, lacked the incentive to do so. Their programs were well-entrenched, financially secure, and change, when experienced, was more likely to be associated with political will than rational planning. As such, computers were considered to be of marginal value. By comparison, the advanced organisations existed within environments of greater uncertainty" (Matheson, 1991: 14).

This is a relatively small-scale study so it would be dangerous to read too much into his findings. Indeed they may need qualifying because he was only investigating a highly specialised and progressive form of computerisation, IT as an aid to strategic planning – a notoriously imprecise endeavour. He was not discussing the more routinised implementations, such as management information systems which we will meet below. Nevertheless, for most social service agencies system implementation, especially on the first occasion, is more akin to innovation than to a routine administrative system enhancement. We will return to the implications of his findings at the end of the chapter.

Computers for Management Purposes – Management Information Systems

The research on the impact of organisational factors upon implementation of strategic planning systems gave us some thought-provoking findings. The research we now give our attention to – the impact on the organisation of the implementation of management information systems – also gives food for thought. This is not so much because the findings are unexpected; it is more that they tend to be downright contradictory. There is contradiction both at a prescriptive level, whether information systems ought or whether they ought not affect the organisation, and at an empirical level, whether they actually do or they do not have an impact on the organisation. Even amongst commentators who agree that there is an impact there is disagreement over what it is and whether it leads to more rational decision-making, or if it merely legitimises what Caputo calls "ideological" decision-making.

First of all: *ought* the management or client information system (MIS) affect the organisational structure? Schoech and Schkade are unequivocal in their insistence that although the system should make the organisation more efficient it should not take it over or distort it. They do admit that this ideal state of affairs only occurs when the IT is in a mature stage of development within the organisation. They posit a six-stage model: initiation; extension; modification; integration; data administration; and, finally, maturity. They claim: "While DP [data processing] changes substantially from Stage 1 to Stage 6, the people, the organisation, the basic organisational decisions, and the information needed to make these decisions are essentially unchanged. That is, the same people need the same information to make the same decisions in the same organisational structure. Thus, as an organisation moves towards maturity, *DP adjusts to accommodate the user, rather than vice versa*" (Schoech and Schkade, 1980: 21) Even though what we have here is a value statement masquerading as a fact, the point should not be lost. IT must be the servant, not the master, of the organisation. It may well be that the logic of IT points to greater efficiency in a change in procedures, but the essential principle is that changes in procedures should only be made to accommodate the logic of IT if the result is better service provision. Procedures should not be changed just to make life easier for the machines if that then leads to life being made more difficult for the people who use them.

Caputo backs up this position, but in so doing he introduces us to a paradox. When a social service organisation is approaching IT maturity its computer systems will be devised to fit into the smooth running of the agency. But to get to this stage Caputo claims that change in thinking about organisations is necessary: "The information system must be revised and adapted until it fits the organisation. This process requires changes both in ways of thinking about organisational structures and functional relationships with other departments or programs" (Caputo, 1988: 103-104).

Other commentators determinedly tell us that IT most certainly should impact upon the organisation. Brinckmann's insistence that service work must be restructured to fit in with the hardware and software offered by the market is the apotheosis of this approach (Brinckmann, 1989). Many other commentators take the line that IT, once introduced, ought to shake up the organisation and make it more rational. But with many of them the line between the moral imperative of "ought" and the rational necessity of a causal link is a very thin one; so we will now turn our attention to views on the logic of IT in the organisation and to empirical studies.

Four major areas have been highlighted in empirical studies of changes which have taken place and in theoretical discussions of their findings. These are: clarity of organisational goals and agency procedures; power; flexibility and autonomy in individual work practices; and legitimacy.

With regard to the fundamental issue of organisational goals, Gandy and Tepperman conclude that the introduction of MIS has led to some clarification of organisational goals, decision criteria and organisational relationships: "Developing an information and evaluation system forces the organization to better define itself and its procedures. Goals and procedures have to be clarified, and programs and services have to be examined as goals are better defined" (Gandy and Tepperman, 1990: 10). Here there is a problem over causality. Certainly we can accept the empirical finding that some goals may have been clarified, but is it possible to jump from this to the conclusion that the organisation is *forced* to better define its own identity? In their defence, they do later qualify this sweeping assertion: "What the literature leaves unclear is the question of whether social service organizations are able to solve these problems of goal definition, information collection and measurement of organisational output. Nor is it clear whether computers simply provide an opportunity and challenge to solve these problems or actually make their solution both more necessary and more difficult" (Gandy and Tepperman, 1990: 11).

After reviewing management computing in the social services in Britain, Lingham and Law came to the conclusion that there is no logical reason for the advent of computerisation to clarify goals and procedures. In an already badly run agency the opposite can happen: "Here computerisation may actually amplify inadequacies of administrative method, with the consequence; bad management out – worse management in! Good computer practice will not improve bad management practice" (Lingham and Law, 1989: 121).

This factor may explain the reluctance to computerise of some of the large agencies in Matheson's study. Perhaps most agencies have less than perfect manual systems and it might be that it takes an innovative individual to overcome the problems inherent in manual records even before tackling the new set of problems created by the introduction of the new technology.

On the equally fundamental issue of power, Caputo gets more deeply enmeshed in his paradox: "As the MIS function is increasingly integrated into the organisation, it requires changes in who makes what kind of decisions" Caputo, 1988: 114). Caputo maintains that it is the computer experts themselves who carve out an empire:

> The MIS function and its staff increasingly permeate the prerogatives of all levels of management: top, middle and operations. Thus, MIS staff influence all levels of management of the organisation, challenging the traditional authority structure. ... In short, the MIS director can come to shape the overall mission of the human service organisation or its ends, as well as the steps the organisation will need to take to carry out its mission (Caputo, 1988: 117-118).

Schoech too, in spite of his and Schkade's hopes mentioned above, identifies potential changes in the authority structure of an organisation following the introduction of a MIS. One of these is similar to Caputo's, although it is expressed in less apocalyptic terms. He merely says that power is gained by those who understand and use the information management system, but he reminds us that this is not the only possible direction in which changes in power can take place. The introduction of a MIS, he claims, leads to an increased centralisation of decision-making, and therefore power. This strengthens the hand of top management (Schoech, 1982). Bronson et al. come to a similar conclusion. They remind us that under a manual system, responsibility for gathering and reporting data is usually distributed across several individuals, but with a computerised system this responsibility is centralised. Therefore control over who gets what information is limited to fewer people (Bronson, Pelz and Trzcinski, 1988: 65).

Kling's exhaustive review of the literature gives a less clear-cut picture. In general he concluded that "computer-based information systems reinforce the structure of power in an organisation simply because computer-based systems are expensive to develop and use. For this reason, top officials who can authorise large expenditures will, on the average, ensure that the expensive analyses serve their interests" (Kling, 1980: 91). But this generality hides some subtle differences, which seem to be related to the size and structure of the organisation.

We heard a lot in Part One about fears over reduction in flexibility and autonomy which might accrue from computerisation. Schoech (1982) claims that decision-making becomes more structured and less flexible because increased information facilitates the focusing, quantification and rationalisation of decisions. Bronson et al. report from their own experience that the advent of more consistent decision rules had an adverse effect on morale: "Under ambiguous decision rules, these workers have considerable discretion, even though the system is inefficient and difficult to document. With decision rules clearly laid out, some discretion enjoyed by support staff is going to be removed and their autonomy reduced. As a result, resentment and turnover may increase" (Bronson, Pelz and Trzcinski, 1988: 65). Kling on the other hand found that attempts to use MIS to monitor staff were not successful: "Many white collar workers attribute job-enlarging rather than job-constricting attributes to the use of automated information systems. ... Workers with some organisational power can effectively resist the attempts of other occupational groups to monitor their work by the use of computerised information systems" (Kling, 1980: 101).

The final big issue which emerges from the scholarly literature – that of legitimacy – is at a theoretical, philosophical, indeed almost metaphysical level in relation to organisations. It is a theme which underpins the whole of Caputo's magnum opus. Put briefly, Caputo claims that the driving force of rationality which lies behind computerisation undermines what he categorises as the indeterminate and ideological nature of social service organisations. Further, he claims that the rationalist *value system* of IT (as he sees it) will challenge the legitimacy of social service values: "On the whole, I contend that an understanding of and an appreciation for computer use and information systems have the potential to alter the bases of power and decision-making authority as they currently exist in an organisation. These may be the least disruptive and, perhaps, the most beneficial consequences of introducing computer use into human service agencies" (Caputo, 1988: 6-7).

It is here that we part company with Caputo. What he categorises as the indeterminate and ideological nature of social service organisations, we see as value systems which are essential to the very nature of social work itself as a professional entity.

There are major research studies which do provide evidence on this subject. First, Gandy and Tepperman (apparently to their disappointment) found that computerisation was hardly anything to write home about in the agencies they had studied: "To conclude, fears about the harmful impacts of computerisation have thus far proved groundless, mere false alarms ... The computer has had little impact, either positive or negative. ... Whether the computer, swallowed whole like a stone, will pass through the system leaving it unchanged or instead disrupt its functioning in serious ways, remains to be seen" (Gandy and Tepperman, 1990: 183). More to the point, Kling's extensive survey found MIS being used more for ideological than "rational" purposes: "When automated data systems are utilised in public policy formation and policy making they appear more as instruments to help actors mobilise support and legitimate their policy preferences than as "decision-making" aids (Kling, 1980: 101).

Conclusions

The organisation and operation of social services agencies is heavily influenced by the views, norms and values of managers and practitioners. This is consistent with the Parsonian Natural-Systems approach. The possible inconsistency in agreement on goals in these types of organisations is consistent with their predominantly professional approach, in which there is constant debate regarding goals and aims, and methods of achieving them.

It is clear that, in relation to resource allocation and systems maintenance or "housekeeping" tasks at least, managers must use the Rational approach. The management level is responsible for the physical survival of the organisation. It is here that we should see routine applications of IT which are relevant to all organisations, for example budget control and human resource management. The operational level in a social service organisation is ideally the most professional (social service) level and it is on this level that the Natural-Systems approach should be most applicable. It is on this level also that IT should be at its most creative.

The strategic planning level is the most problematic. Strategic planning is an imaginative and creative process, supra-rational rather than irrational. Perhaps this squares the circle and legitimates the individualism and charisma which seem to be necessary here. Even Weber accepted that decision-making and planning at the highest level about the very future of the bureaucracy are undertaken outside the range of the rules of the bureaucracy itself. It is here on the strategic planning level that IT is at its most primitive stage.

How do we reconcile the Natural Systems approach on the operational level with the Rational approach on the management level? This is an issue in most social service organisations. We constantly hear the complaints of social workers who have to fill out all those reports for the managers, thereby reducing the amount of time they have to work with their clients. IT can facilitate this integration process if it is introduced with imagination and with sensitivity to the needs of both groups. In IT practice this means: the managers say to the social workers. "Social workers 'do your thing' but use IT to do it. And, while your at it, build into your IT system something for us. Then we will both be happy".

The Rational (mechanistic) and Natural Systems (organic) approaches operate differentially at different levels of the organisation. At the operational level the organic approach is epitomised in social work practice. It is flexible and humanistic and needs, normally, a creative IT approach. On the other hand much work at the operational level is routine: filing, information searching, legal, welfare rights etc., which calls for routinised IT. At the management level most of the day-to-day work will be routinised and easily amenable to the mechanistic aspects of IT, so long as it does not make too many organisational waves or disrupt the "real" channels of communication and control – i.e. the informal mechanisms.

CHAPTER 5

Policy Issues

Now that we have explored the conceptual and organisational issues related to IT in the social services, the time has come to investigate the mechanisms through which it is implemented and developed. We start by looking at the policy process and then investigate in some detail an example of policy change where IT is central: the emergence of Case Management as an important new type of social work practice. Finally we tell a cautionary tale about that crucial issue in policy-making – power. We will see that the introduction of IT is often related more to agency power politics than to the logic of system design

IT and the Policy Process

Policy gives direction towards the accomplishment of some purpose or goal by requiring the implementation of a pattern of actions. This precludes discrete and unrelated decisions and actions by unco-ordinated individuals (Anderson, 1975). Policy-making is understood primarily in terms of the making of choices about *what* is to be achieved and *how* it is to be effected (Berman and Phillips, 1994). Therefore, policy-making relates directly to organisational, informational and political conditions within which choices are made (Nakamura, 1987). Radford (1978) presents three functional levels of operation within an organisation which are related to the development and implementation of policy: the strategic planning level, which is concerned with the formulation of objectives and policies of the organisation and changes in objectives and resources; the management level, which is concerned with the effective use of resources in order to reach organisational objectives; and the operational level, which carries out the specific tasks of the organisation. Each functional level uses information and data to a different degree and in a different fashion.

Webb and Wistow (1986) use a similar framework but they formulate it in terms of "policy streams" instead of "levels". Their three policy streams are as follows:

1) *governance policies* which specify the general view taken of the role of the state as well as the philosophy of management and control to be adopted within public authorities;

2) *resource policies* which specify broad patterns of expenditure, detailed allocations between competing uses, and the dominant approaches taken in resource management;

3) *service or output policies* which specify the social needs to be met and the choice of appropriate means and methods of intervention.

The notion of streams is more dynamic than that of levels; streams can interact, compete and be in conflict with each other. An approach based on policy streams is more untidy than one based on the more straightforward concept of levels but it is of greater use in that it more adequately reflects the real world of social service organisations.

IT and Policy Streams: an Example

Eaglstein and Berman (1993) report on a study exploring the tensions between different policy streams (particularly resource and service policy streams) associated with IT implementation in the Israeli Ministry of Labour and Social Affairs. The Ministry is the agent of central government which determines social policy, initiates legislation and enacts regulations for social service delivery which is carried out by the local authorities. The study compares the use of, and the attitudes towards, computers among the ministry's department administrators and its national supervisors.

The division of labour between departmental administrators and national supervisors is clear. Department administrators are responsible for the administration of services and resource control, personnel and budget. National supervisors are responsible for the implementation and supervision of social services according to the ministry's social work guidelines. In other words, the department administrators are responsible for the resource policy stream whereas the national supervisors are responsible for the service policy stream.

The computerisation policy of the Ministry since its inception has clearly placed priority on resources rather than outputs. Emphasis has been placed upon the development of IT programmes which are related to the transfer of financial payments to outside agencies. The agencies provide services such as day care and residential care for children, the aged and other populations; medical payments for the needy; and social service personnel. These services make up the major financial expense and the major financial output of various departmental budgets of the social affairs section of the ministry, therefore demanding the administrators' utmost attention. Resource policy has priority in the competition of computerisation resources. The national supervisors do not have access to specialised computerised programming. They are dependent on paper reporting from the field and use the computer only for the administrative aspects of their tasks.

The consequences of this policy were as follows:

1) Department administrators report a more positive attitude towards the computer than national supervisors. For example, department administrators demonstrate greater interest in learning more about the computer and its uses, report greater satisfaction in the use of the computer, feel that the computer gives them job independence, are more positive regarding the service they receive from the computer department, and report a more positive image of their department as a result of the use of the computer than national supervisors.
2) Department administrators make greater use of the computer than the national supervisors. Computer programmes are more available to the department administrators across all programme categories.
3) Department administrators feel that the computer has greater impact on their work than the national supervisors. The department administrators deal with resources, therefore it is expected that since the computer policy of the ministry is resource-oriented, the computer programmes will have a greater impact on the tasks of the department administrators than the supervisors.
4) Department administrators were more involved in the development of departmental computer programmes and received over 100% more training in the use of the computer than the national supervisor.

Eaglstein and Berman demonstrate that the domination of one policy stream impacts on the implementation of programmes at the cost of other policy streams. Because the computer policy of the Ministry is resource-oriented the computer programmes have a greater impact on the tasks of the department administrators who deal with resources. In their case, control of resources has priority over the control of people even in a people-processing organisation. Once the computer programmes controlling resources were in place the programming in the area of resource policy continued to receive priority to the access of IT services at the cost of service policy personnel.

This is a salutary tale. It is a classic example of "to him who hath it shall be given". As has happened so often in social services agencies, computerisation has begun in the finance department and has spread to financial (and therefore resource) administrators. This has given power to administration rather than to service delivery. It is clear that the national supervisors have been frozen out. And it is the national supervisors who are the link between national policy-making and the local provision of social work services and therefore who are the workers at national level who are closest to the social workers themselves.

Two general points can be taken from this example. The first concerns the setting of precedents. The policy stream which gets in first is able to set the agenda in terms of both the type of information which is gathered and its "locus". If a resource policy stream dominates then the highest priority in the information system will go to the collection and analysis of data on resources, whereas if a service policy stream dominates then priority goes to collection and analysis of data on outputs. The locus of information (Swanson, 1978) refers to its location within the organisational framework and who has control over it.

The second relates to the interaction between policy streams. Intrinsically the service delivery policy stream has less power than the resource policy stream but they are so intertwined, particularly in terms of organisational informational needs, that service delivery is not a lost cause. Things *could* have been different for Eaglstein and Berman's national supervisors if they had played their cards better.

Governance Policy, IT and Inter-Organisation Oriented Social Services Agencies

As we saw in Chapter 3 social service agencies are highly dependent on resources controlled by other agencies and operate very much within an inter-agency context. Hence they must operate within an open and interactive governance policy. Some agencies in particular function in a situation of total interdependence with other agencies and these have special IT needs in relation to their governance policies. Such an agency could be a social service organisation working within a country-wide social service delivery system (Highfill, Mundle, Page and Armentrout, 1986), a social service integration project (State Reorganization Commission, 1989), an integrated family services system (Oklahoma Department of Human Services, 1989) or a multi-service centre (Sircar, Schkade and Schoech, 1983). Such networks of interdependent agencies require an integrated information system with full coordination on a wide range of issues, including protocols for gathering information, policy parameters, and the nature of inter-organisational interaction (Challis, 1988). Sircar, Schkade and Schoech (1983) report that the multi-service centre incorporates such features as: a common or compatible definition of services; uniform intake procedures; sharing of data across services; and a central planning, managing and controlling body.

Extensive networking is central to any decentralised inter-organisational social service delivery system. Consensus-building and cooperation at all levels is critical to the success of an IT project that includes diverse policy-making groups and a wide variety of public and private service providers. Particular attention also needs to be given to system development. Highfill, Mundle, Page and Armentrout (1986) denote eight steps for implementing an integrated information management system used by a large consortium of public and private service agencies:

1) Identification of the questions that decision-makers most urgently need answered in order to make resource allocation decisions.
2) Identification of the type and amount of data necessary to answer each of those questions.
3) Identification of the client data already being collected by the social service agencies.
4) Identification of techniques required to construct and maintain the client database.
5) Estimation of resources required to establish and maintain the information management system.
6) Identification of agencies whose participation in the information management system would be appropriate.
7) Confirmation at decision-maker workshops that such coordinated information management is desirable and feasible.
8) Undertaking of community surveys and creation of social indicators to provide additional information on needs and service effectiveness.

At a less grand level there is much scope for cooperative measures to deal with duplication in the provision of services: "computerised information and referral systems have been the most common solution for this problem. A somewhat expanded version of these systems are client tracking systems, such as those in Broward County, Florida and Kansas City, Missouri. These schemes allow for client-related information to be shared on an area-wide basis, and have the potential for ensuring that scarce resources are utilised most effectively" (Butterfield, 1986: 11).

Policy Change and IT

The replacement of one policy or programme by another directed at the same problem and/or clientele is called policy succession. Hogwood and Peters (1982) claim that the implementation of policy succession demonstrates a need to alter or consolidate existing organisational structures, to resocialise existing personnel, and to adapt operating rules for the new policy. These three factors all have an impact on an IT system.

The Coming of Case Management

A study of policy succession within the English social services provides an example of how different social service policies influence the conception and design of an IT programme. One can identify a progression of three distinct and clearly defined social service policies in England since the 1960s. While all three were based around service delivery by the local authority Social Services Departments, each reflected alternative conceptual approaches to social service delivery.

The first, the "social service delivery system" in the 1960s and early 1970s, was highly centralised. This was followed by the "community social work" or "patch-work" system which represented a decentralised client-oriented social service delivery approach. Finally, the Government White Paper *Caring for People: Community Care in the Next Decade and Beyond* (1989), instituted market-ori-ented "Case Management" as national policy. The case management approach was implemented via a succession of Acts of Parliament. There is a financial incentive for local authorities to use their resources to fund and contract with external agen-cies (Glennerster, Power and Travers, 1991). So, the devolution of service admin-istration became an integral part of case management.

Each of the above social service delivery policies require different IT system design approaches. The change from one social service delivery policy to another requires changes in the conceptual approach to the IT system, its design, informa-tion requirements and locus of power as can be seen from the following:

Policy	*Information System*
Centralised	Information service by service
	Management needs predominate
	Centralised service administration
Patchwork	Client and neighbourhood centred database
	Practitioner/manager needs predominate
	Decentralised service administration
Case Management	Client and service delivery centred database
	Case manager needs predominate
	Service networking

Under the centralised service-oriented there was no standardised information trans-fer between services for children, people with mental health problems, people with disabilities and older people. The "patchwork" decentralised policy focused on the neighbourhood. It required an information system covering: facilities in the local community (voluntary, informal and statutory); services available from the "patch" team; and the client's needs. The Case Management approach requires extensive net-working between an integrated client database, a service provision database, a fi-nancial management system and a decentralised administrative information system.

Case Management in Practice

Case management is such a radical departure from the status quo that it is worth investigating it in some detail. First of all we need to say precisely what it is. Case management can be defined as a method of delivering social services where a person or team takes full responsibility for delivery and coordination (but not necessarily the actual provision) of services after developing an appropriate service plan in consultation with the client (and often the client's family). It is the case manager's duty to ensure access to services, to monitor service delivery, and to evaluate service outcomes. Weil, Kails and Associates classify case management as having a co-ordinating function with therapeutic facets: "The essential elements of case management are client identification, assessment of need, service planning, service coordination and linking, and the monitoring and continuous evaluation of the client, of service delivery, and of available resources" (1988: 3). In the family context, case management is the brokering and coordinating of the multiple social, health, education and employment services necessary to promote self-sufficiency and strengthen family life.

As a method of social work intervention, case management is still in its early stages of development. Little was heard about it before the mid-1970s. The term "case managers" appeared for the first time in *Social Work Abstracts* in January, 1985. Its emergence as a distinct concept was linked to the growth of social service programmes during the 1960s in the United States. Public funding for those service programmes was previously provided largely through channels with responsibility for funding individual client groups only, resulting in a highly complex, fragmented, and uncoordinated network of services with considerable overlap and duplication. During the early 1970s, the Department of Health, Education and Welfare funded a series of demonstration projects to test various approaches to improve the coordination of federal service programmes at the state and local levels. These "service integration" projects featured such techniques as client tracking systems, one-stop service centres, specialised management information systems, inter-agency planning and service delivery agreements, computerised resource inventories and management reorganisation projects (National Association of Social Workers, 1987b).

The implementation of case management necessitates a thorough reorganisation in the social service delivery system process. It also requires a familiarity with computerised information systems (Grisham, White and Miller, 1983). While it is technically possible to implement case management without using IT it only becomes a fully viable social service delivery strategy when it is based upon a computerised information system (Chubon, 1986). Blazyk, Wimberley and Crawford (1987) note that there is a natural affinity between case management and computer-based information systems, and that a management information system is required to assist a case manager to monitor the caseload and the work undertaken by the providers. Streatfield (1992) claims that the British community case management legislation creates demands which cannot be met by traditional working practices. Adequate information systems are indispensable and only computerised systems will fit the bill.

Well, what is it that case managers have to do? Flynn and Miller (1991: 2) summarise the British Government's requirements for case management under the *National Health Service and Community Care Act 1990*:

1) Case management is a means of achieving a better fit between services and individual needs.
2) It involves: the assessment of individual need; the design, with the client and carers, of a package of care; the purchase of that package; and its monitoring and review.
3) Case managers are the front line of inter-agency collaboration enabling complementary services such as health to be integrated into an overall package of care.
4) Case management through assessment, purchasing and monitoring has a major role to play in quality assurance.
5) Case management is an important mechanism for identifying unmet needs and ways in which presently serviced needs can be better met and hence is an essential ingredient in community care planning and service development.
6) Devolved resource management (management in which the authority and accountability for service delivery and finance and personnel are devolved from the "Headquarters" to a level closer to the point of service delivery) is an important means of enabling case managers to work flexibly with clients.

Case Management and IT

We will use two examples to see how IT can help case managers to do their job. The first is the AIDS Project Los Angeles (APLA) which has developed a case management programme designed to increase access to services for people with AIDS (Sonsel, Paradise and Stroup, 1988). Social workers are the primary case managers, with volunteer groups serving as "extenders" in maintaining client contact, assessing clients' ongoing needs, conducting intakes, and providing medical transportation. The second is a computerised case management system developed at the University of Texas Medical Branch for the Houston-Galveston Area Agency on Ageing (Wimberly and Blazyk, 1989). It is a hospital-based programme designed to assist elderly patients in locating and using community resources.

In both case management systems a computer-assisted approach was used to do the following: maintain a client database; undertake client tracking; maintain a resource data bank; make comprehensive use of referral resources through the coordination of services; match identified client needs with data bank information on resources; and monitor staff activities such as the authorisation of expenditures. Both sets of authors report a string of successes in increasing efficiency: faster delivery of services; increased number of relevant referrals; improved service coordination; more effective monitoring of services and care plans; better evaluation of needs; provision of accurate and timely statistical reports, trend analysis and resource information; and reduction in paperwork and in personnel costs (Sonsel, Paradise and Stroup, 1988; Wimberly and Blazyk, 1989).

The effective use of information was central to these efficiency gains. A social service agency cannot effectively apply case management as a service delivery system without reviewing, evaluating and reprogramming its information processing capability. The effective development of case management as a social service delivery system goes with the development of the various IT systems needed to carry it out. Finally, and this is a most important implication, the social services have entered the world of technology by integrating IT concepts in the development of a relevant social service strategy.

Power Politics and System Implementation

The stakes here are very high because in this case study the plan was to establish a computer system to allocate resources between all the social services departments in Israel, and the resources which were to be allocated were the most crucial of all – social work staff (Berman, 1992). So, individuals' jobs were on the line here.

In the past, social work staff resources were distributed to the municipal social services departments on the basis of two criteria. The first was political pressure: those mayors and/or directors of social service departments who were closer to the political "pot" were able to pressure decision-makers in the Ministry of Labour and Social Affairs to allot additional social workers. The second criterion was the perceived efficient use of resources. This led to a programming where the "rich get richer and the poor got poorer". The social service departments receiving additional personnel were usually the larger ones from the big cities. They were able to recruit the best social workers. The "poor" social service departments from the outlying areas, small towns, development towns and regional councils were not able to recruit the better social workers. Therefore, though their "social needs" might have been greater their inability to plan good programmes prevented them from attaining additional social work staff.

The newly implemented personnel allocation system changed the rules of the game in the relationship between the municipalities, social service departments and the Ministry of Labour and Social Affairs. Once the criteria for social work personnel allocation are determined political pressure plays a diminishing role. The political impact is transferred to the process of deciding what sort of data should be used to create the variables in the programme. Social service directors who have an interest in the distribution of social work personnel need to know what the impact of the specific variables will be on the final decision. The decision therefore is no longer who you know but what you know, i.e. which of the variables in the pro-gramme will operate to your own political advantage.

Setting up the Programme

The construction of the programme drew heavily upon work undertaken in Israel to identify reliable personnel allocation methods based upon objective measures (Pardes, 1977, 1978; Eaglstein and Pardes, 1983). These included the level of prevailing community distress and population size. Seven variables were identi-fied as measuring the level of community distress: percentage of families with three or more children; percentage of persons aged 65 or more in the population; de-pendency ratio; rate of children aged below 18 placed in institutions; crime rate; local taxes per capita; rate of vehicle ownership (Pardes, 1977, 1978). For rural communities, distance from a main metropolitan area is also included in the for-mula (Eaglstein and Pardes, 1983). This method enabled the Ministry of Labour and Social Affairs to allocate social work personnel on the basis of objective data. The computer analysed the data and determined the social work personnel distri-bution to the social service departments on the basis of the formula.

One positive outcome was that the results were seen as impartial and not cor-rupted by special pleading or political power. Ministry of Labour and Social Affairs decision-makers answered the queries of the social service departments who were not happy with their allocation by saying: "the computer determined what you get". Unfortunately the negative outcome was a consensus that the results were wrong. They did not match up with common sense perceptions of which were the most needy areas. While there was general agreement that the method of using objec-tive criteria in a computerised decision support system was correct, the relation-ship between the variables in the formula was incorrect. In reality the level of prevailing community distress and population size (which was used inversely: larger cities receiving proportionately fewer social workers) was skewed in favour of the smaller socially distressed towns. Large cities with average levels of distress but with large distressed inner-city neighbourhoods did not receive needed social work personnel.

There was increasing pressure to change the variables in the application of the personnel decision support system and inevitably a committee was formed. The role of the committee was to determine which variables were to be included. The committee membership represented a wide spectrum of political interests in the social work personnel allocation and implementation process. It included the director of the division of personal social services who is responsible for the delivery of social services on the municipal level, the directors of the three administrative districts of the Ministry of Labour and Social Affairs (Tel Aviv, Jerusalem and Haifa), two department directors of social services and a social planner whose role was adviser to the committee.

The decision on which variables were to be included in the decision support system demanded that the participants, all social work professionals, played a role strange to them. They were required to determine which variables should be included in a decision support system and would therefore impact on social work personnel allocation. At one point in their discussions they turned to the social planner and said: "you work it out on the computer and you decide". But eventually they were convinced that ultimately personnel allocation decisions are political decisions. Therefore it is not computers but policy-makers who must decide on the criteria which will be used in the computer system.

After much discussion and many computer simulations three variables were identified as adequately reflecting different political criteria for personnel allocation in the social services in Israel. Each provided an alternative method of measuring the personnel needs in social service departments. The first variable is the percentage of the population known to the local social service department. The measure per city is derived by dividing the number of persons known to the social service department by the population of the city.

The second variable is the average number of treatment hours invested by the social workers per case. This variable is a measurement of the intensity of the problems of each case at the social service department. The social worker identifies the problems of a family (case) from a list of 37 problem types used by all social service departments and classifies the treatment status of the family as either under periodic review, or care at a low level of intensity or care at a high level of intensity. An expert committee assigns proposed hours of treatment per year for each type of problem by treatment status ranging from a minimum of 5 hours (periodic review) to a maximum of 150 hours (for example, a drug user with care at a high level of intensity). The number of treatment hours per social service department is then calculated. This figure is divided by the number of files in the social service department, providing the average number of treatment hours needed by the social worker per case. The third variable is the socio-economic index (community distress) of the city. This variable measures the potential population who are candidates for services at the social service department. The index used is a socio-economic index based on a factor analysis of 34 variables from the Israeli census of 1983 (Ben-Tuvia, Deychev and Dor, 1988).

Implementation

This is where political considerations became central. The Ministry of Labour and Social Affairs is divided into three administrative districts and each district has very different characteristics in relation to the three chosen variables in deciding personnel allocation. The districts are: Jerusalem and South Israel, Haifa and North Israel, and the Tel Aviv and Central district. The Tel Aviv and Central district is made up mainly of large cities and is the major conurbation of Israel. It contains

45% of the total Israeli population. The Jerusalem and Haifa districts each include one large city, a number of smaller cities and some small development towns which had very high levels of deprivation and "community distress".

Haifa district has a much larger number of development towns than Jerusalem and because of this it argued for maintenance of the status quo in using variable number three, the socio-economic (community distress) index, to measure social worker personnel allocations.

The Jerusalem district preferred variable number one, the percentage of population known to the social service departments, because 14.1% of its population was known to the social service departments; a higher percentage than the other two districts. Yet the Jerusalem district was willing to compromise to combine the community distress variables (the Jerusalem district has 14 development towns) with the percentage of the population known to the social service departments. This would, for the Jerusalem district, mean the best of two worlds.

The Tel Aviv district argued otherwise. It includes only five development towns, and the lowest percentage of the population known to the social service departments. It has a large urban and economic base. The Tel Aviv district argued in favour of a variant of the second variable – the *total* (not average) number of hours of treatment as the variable to use in social worker personnel allocation. The Tel Aviv district uses 64% of all treatment person-hours, and invests the highest number of hours per social problem. These figures indicate a greater intensity of social problems (e.g. drug addiction, alcoholism, family problems), a phenomenon common to the inner cities.

The fundamental issue was to decide which of the three variables or combination of variables would be best in a decision support system (DSS) for allocating social worker personnel resources. But this issue cannot be resolved impartially and objectively. In the end it is a choice between different conceptions of need which in practical terms will be influenced by considerations of self-interest and expediency. It is not surprising, therefore, that the solution finally reached by the personnel allocation committee was a compromise. The DSS included a combination of the "community distress" variable, the existing variable in use, with the average number of treatment hours invested by the social worker per case.

This case-study forcibly reminds us that it is not possible to find technical solutions to political problems. A logical system can clarify the bases upon which decisions are made but cannot overcome irreconcilable differences about the relative merits of different assessment criteria.

Conclusions

Political problems do not have technical solutions but IT can be, and regrettably often is, used for political purposes in decision-making. Avoiding this requires vigilance from professionals with the ability to straddle the interface of policy and technology. Once policy goals are agreed, though, IT can be used to enhance existing policies, as in inter-organisational co-operation. In some circumstances it can even enable the development of policies which would be impracticable without IT, such as case management.

Even after it has been implemented, IT can result in a major – and often unforeseen – impact on policy. This occurs when it is expropriated by specific interest groups who use IT as a resource to achieve their sectional goals at the expense of other legitimate goals of other groups within the social services organisation. In this way IT can be misused to gain or maintain power in the policy-making process.

PART III

IT IN PRACTICE

Chapter 6

Issues in the Implementation of IT

It is not our intention to provide a recipe on how to introduce computers into a social service agency. That has been done very well elsewhere (Bronson, Pelz and Trzcinski, 1988; Schoech, 1982 and, 1990). Rather, what we want to do is to introduce general themes which will inform and guide the reader through the implementation process. We start with a vital question: is the agency ready to computerise? This is followed by a discussion of strategies which are crucial in the IT process: successful staff involvement; the proper use of IT experts; and resource allocation. We then discuss some practical issues in IT implementation including the crucial issues of information needs, information control and screen design. Finally we give an illustration of an IT programme designed to monitor a client's progress.

Readiness and Commitment

The first point to make is that computerisation takes a long time to come to fruition, and during this period the agency has precious little to show for its pains. Caputo (1988) tells us that a social service agency must go through a long, tedious and frustrating process of adapting a data processing system to the organisation and the user if it is to be successful. Schoech, Schkade and Mayers (1981) report that the completion of the process of introducing an IT subsystem in a relatively small agency may take more than a year. Bronson et al. (1988) describe a package which took 25 months to implement. Their first piece of advice once an agency has started to computerise is a sobering reminder that timetables for implementing computerisation normally overrun. "As a rule of thumb, after you have worked out a careful estimate of how long each phase will take, *double the estimate* and you may come close to reality" (1988: 18, emphasis in original). They also rather ruefully tell us in the epilogue to their study, when they had the benefit of seeing all that had gone wrong: "Expect an extended period of frustration and confusion, especially on software programs that are not adopted ready-made like word processing, but have to be adapted or heavily customised. As the business manager [on one of their projects] said of the accounting programme: 'Whatever could have gone wrong did'" (1988: 142). They report that about half the pilot programmes had to be redesigned. They estimate that it takes two years or more before the first application can be securely in place.

The next issue is whether the agency is ready for computerisation. The importance of assessing the readiness of the organisation for computerisation should not be underestimated. It includes the evaluation of staff support, organisational problems, and resources (including time and organisational stability). Success in even the preliminary stage requires the full support of the staff. If the agency has organisational problems it is probably better to postpone computerisation until the difficulties are resolved. In addition, the transition to a computerised information system requires a great deal of time and effort that may have to be appropriated from other organisational tasks. To implement a successful system, the organisation must be able to withstand a temporary decrease in attention in these other areas. For this reason, Bronson et al. (1988) recommend that the IT process be implemented only if the agency is in a relatively stable period. It needs to be able to withstand the stress of organisational change, and to adjust to changes in its structure of power and discretion.

A factor which is perhaps more important than even organisational readiness is the presence of an individual with adequate power within the organisation who has unflagging enthusiasm and commitment to champion the implementation process and to ensure that it is followed through successfully. Gandy and Tepperman (1990), along with other commentators, argue strongly that this is the major factor contributing to the success of implementation of large-scale computerisation. Bronson et al. (1988) go even further. They point out that like any other organisational innovation, the survival of a computerised information system will be in question when a high-level executive or other key backer of the system leaves, so they advise that there should be two or three respected people committed to the project in case one of them departs. Even this may not be enough. British research has indicated that there also needs to be strong commitment at middle management level, as well as at the head of the agency, in order to ensure smooth and successful implementation (Forrest and Williams, 1987).

A delicate balance must be kept between commitment and expertise. In the early stages at least it is unlikely that there will be anyone in the agency with sufficient technical expertise to oversee the day-to-day implementation. Consequently it makes sense to hire a competent external consultant to deal with technical matters while the manager who is committed to implementation can concentrate on strategic issues. But, within a few years the role of the outside consultant should be

taken on by someone on the agency's staff. By that time the IT should have become bedded down within the organisation.

The next crucial large-scale issue is that of effective, but flexible, planning. This
needs to be done through a task force or steering committee (Schoech, 1982) and
must include long-term planning for staff training and reorientation (Hammer and
Hile, 1985; Sharkey, 1989; Marsh, Omerod and Roberts, 1986). An implementation plan should be initiated before computers are introduced into the organisation. Such a plan should identify specific long-term and short-term goals and
potential benefits for staff and clients.

Staff Involvement

It is essential that this planning is genuinely participatory: "Administrators who
fail to involve the staff in planning for the introduction of computers do so at great
risk of failure. At best, they will generate indifference, avoidance and resentment.
At worst, they may create stolid opposition and subterfuge" (Gandy and Tepperman,
1990: 186). Staff involvement needs to be a continuous process from the initial
thinking stages right through to the time when the system is fully up and running.
One finds that virtually all commentators agree with Gandy and Tepperman in
insisting on the necessity of wide-scale staff involvement. There is a dissenting
voice, however, from Romano, Conklin and Fisher (1985). They reason that the
main argument for absolute managerial autocracy as opposed to full participatory
involvement is in the limitations of time. They warn us that if critical decisions
must be made in hours rather than days, participatory democracy may not be
advisable. Furthermore, they say that even the most limited forms of participation
may be a bad idea: "If pressures for staff productivity are such that virtually 100
percent of staff time must be available for patient care in order to preserve the
integrity of departmental program / existence, then even limited staff participation
may not be indicated or possible". These recommendations, we believe, are a recipe
for absolute disaster.

Involvement of staff at all relevant levels of the agency is not just a first priority:
it is an absolute principle. From our own personal experiences, from discussion
with people who have implemented IT in the social services and from most of the
literature we have searched, the message is the same – if you don't consult effectively then in all probability things will go dramatically wrong.

Staff involvement is multi-faceted. It includes input regarding both the technical and humanistic aspects of computerisation. Schoech (1982) found that the typical
organisation will spend almost all its time on the technological aspects of a computer application, whereas one of the areas that need most attention is that of human
factors: people's adjustment to change. The introduction of IT into a social service
agency is a social change process and has its greatest impact on people. Workers

in social service agencies often believe that the introduction of IT into an agency will lead to a reduction in interpersonal dialogue, an increasingly authoritarian style of management, and a loss of democratic ideals (Karger and Kreuger, 1988). There can also be a perception that the values of IT represent the antithesis of the values of social work. Lack of staff readiness for IT is likely to have a highly negative impact on morale, turnover and organisational effectiveness (Kucic, Sorensen and Hanbery, 1983). Koroloff (1989) found that once the IT process is being implemented the potential for staff resistance and disruption of work with IT is high.

Implementing organisational change includes the diffusion of new knowledge within the organisation. Backer (1991) states that everyone who will have to live with the results of an organisational change needs to be involved in planning for innovation, both to get a range of suggestions for how to undertake it effectively and to facilitate "felt ownership" of the new programme (thus decreasing resistance to change). The greater the involvement of workers or other stakeholders in planning the coming change, the better their chances of accepting it (Glaser, Abelson and Garrison, 1983). The ultimate success of the diffusion of IT in an organisation is heavily dependent on the initial and continued support of its users (Mandell, 1989).

Effective involvement is particularly crucial when the process is first initiated. Hammer and Hile (1985) conclude that the initial involvement of end-users including social workers and clerical officers in goal setting, system design and decision-making in the implementation phases is a crucial variable in later acceptance of the IT system. As many workers as possible should be involved in the IT process in order to enlist their support for its utilisation as early as possible (Sullivan, 1980; Wodarski, 1988).

Bronson et al. insist that good communications are vital to effective staff involvement. Staff can benefit from the computer, but one must ensure that they know how and when these benefits will occur. They suggest:

> Keep staff members informed of the decision to computerise, assure them that their jobs are not jeopardised, emphasise that their inputs at the system design stage are important, and try to ensure that everyone has something to gain from the new system. Each of these steps will contribute to a better reception when the computer arrives on the scene (1988: 19).

Newkham and Bawcom (1981) in reporting on the implementation of an integrated clinical and financial information system note that the involvement of staff from the beginning of the project enhanced communication at all locations. Unexpectedly positive results occurred simply because accurate and complete information was available, along with an enabling managerial atmosphere. Staff relations improved as their energy was directed towards the agency goal of providing service.

Initiation into the realm of IT can be very daunting and may seem to involve entirely new skills – the social worker is being asked to be involved in introducing "technology" into a "human" service setting. Yet dealing with social change is part of the everyday work of social workers and the introduction of new technology is just one aspect of social change. So social workers are already equipped with the know-how and skills to introduce IT in a social service organisation. The secret of successful implementation is to deal with the process from a social change perspective, which social workers can of course comfortably handle, and not to try to deal with it from a technical perspective. A classic example of these two different approaches was given in Mutschler and Cnaan's 1985 study of two agencies in Israel which we discussed in Chapter 2.

Overcoming Resistance to Computerisation

In Chapter 1 we looked at reasons for resistance to computerisation among social workers. We now identify a number of ways to overcome it. For all the limitations of their research findings, Gandy and Tepperman (1990), exhibit much wisdom on this subject, which is best expressed in their own words:

> It is probably safest for a manager implementing computerization to assume that covert resistance will occur unless prevented and will continue until remedied. The way to prevent it is through cooperative planning and open discussion of the consequences of the new technology for every aspect of work. Assume that what is not discussed openly will be discussed secretly or, at least, feared in private. Probably prevention is better than remedy and may be the sane course to take: namely, open discussion and a genuine willingness to accept input from all levels of staff. Initial uses of computers for management and administration tend to let direct service staff imagine that computer technology has little value for their day-to-day work. Once computers are identified to be no more than management tools, staff will show little interest in looking for and undertaking other, and more creative uses. Organizations should simultaneously implement technology that will meet some information needs of all levels of staff (Gandy and Tepperman, 1990: 187).

This brings to mind Williams and Forrest's admonition to managers in a slightly different but related context: "Managers will ... need to learn to use, not abuse, the values and culture of social work" (1988: 218).

Within this general category of resistance to computers it is worth reviewing Karger and Kreuger's recommendations. They are highly sceptical about new technology and their approach is imbued with a deep mistrust. Nevertheless, some of their recommendations are very pertinent. As well as agreeing with the virtually universal recommendation that all relevant workers should be allowed to participate in the decision-making process and making the sensible suggestion that workers unable to get on with the technology should have the right to move to a non-computerised job, they introduce two new objectives for managers to strive towards:

Banning Technospeak: This is an entirely laudable aim: "Technical specialists should be forced to speak in English sentences. Moreover, technocrats should be charged with translating the non-ordinary language of symbolic logic and technical argot into everyday office vernacular. The responsibility for presenting the "technological subuniverse of meaning" to the rest of the world should be lodged with those who advocate the use of computers" (Karger and Kreuger, 1988: 123).

Enforcing the "Pareto Optimum": This is the ultimate acid test for computerisation. "No policy, program, or office activity should be undertaken unless it can be demonstrated in advance to help at least one person and harm no one. If such a condition cannot be guaranteed then a proposed technological change should be delayed" (ibid.). In fact, the "harm no one clause" is a tough one. A less stringent formulation would insist on a Benthamite calculus where overall utility would be enhanced and any diswelfares would be fully compensated. But irrespective of its formulation, the principle is vital, and it is regrettably true that some of the less well thought-through and underplanned computer implementations ended up helping no one in the agencies (although they boosted the profits in the hardware trade) and produced considerable diswelfares.

How Experts Should be Used

Schoech reports that the process of implementing IT programmes in the social services is difficult, frustrating and problematic. He raises the issue of the type of personnel needed in accompanying a computerisation process. Much of the literature refers to the presence of an IT "expert" or consultant (Schoech, 1979; Schoech, Schkade and Mayers, 1981; Sircar, Schkade and Schoech, 1983; de Graaf, 1987; Rowley, 1990). In the initial stages of the IT process the "expert", the IT professional, plays an important role in introducing IT. Inevitably, this expert is an outsider. (It is only at a much later stage, when IT is in place in the social service organisation that one can assume that there will be an "insider" IT expert.) We use Ross's (1967) community organisation perspective in relation to three possible scenarios in the introduction of programmes by external agents in an IT setting.

Scenario 1: the Expert is in Control – The IT expert diagnoses the social service organisation's needs, prescribes the necessary hardware and software and then seeks to implement the plan.

Here the IT expert is invited by management to make a systems analysis, present an IT plan to the staff and implement that plan within the social service agency without any staff involvement. The IT expert's plan comes from the outside and is imposed on the social service organisation. The expert's self-perception is as someone who knows best. In this scenario Boguslaw's (1981) view of system designers and computer programmers is that they possess power in that they are in control of the system. The interaction between the expert and the staff is imposed by management. The role of staff is to serve the expert. The staff's input into the development of the IT programme is through the expert who has the final decision regarding the design and implementation of the IT programme. Staff, on the other hand, have no direct input. The expert's dominant role in designing an IT plan for a social service agency will tend to alienate social workers whose value system instinctively comes into conflict with IT normative expectations. It is under these circumstances that there is a feeling on the part of social workers that technological rationality is invading the domain of human discourse. This type of plan implementation is often doomed to failure with the IT system quickly falling into disuse.

Scenario 2: the Expert Persuades – After diagnosing the social service organisation's needs and prescribing hardware and software, the IT expert then attempts to persuade the staff that the IT plan should be implemented.

Here the social service staff are a passive audience to which a product is being sold. The staff evaluate a finished product in whose development they had no involvement. The social processes involved are similar to Scenario 1. The IT expert attempts to communicate with the staff only after the deed is done. Within a social service agency this type of communication is usually self-defeating. The IT expert must recognise that communication is the basis of the social service process (LaMendola, Glastonbury and Toole, 1989). In this scenario the IT expert is demonstrating to social workers the inevitability of their greatest fear that the computer is an impediment to the communication process including that between social worker and client. In this scenario the use of IT in the social service organisation depends on the selling ability of the IT expert and not necessarily on the soundness and relevance of the system. The social service staff feel no personal identification with the product.

Scenario 3: Genuine Staff Involvement – The IT expert involves the social service staff in the initial stages of the IT process. At this stage the staff will be consulted on their views and canvassed about possible amendments and extension of the programme to help them perform their jobs better.

A principal aim here is to make the service recipients part of the process by which the service is formulated (Grosser, 1973). This can be seen as self-determination, as opposed to outside or even management control. In this scenario the staff feel that they have participated in the development of the IT programme.

They have a stake in its operational success. It is this type of expert/staff relationship which fosters the greatest success in the implementation of IT in a social service agency.

According to Ross, what would be needed in the successful introduction and implementation of IT into a social service setting is the realisation of the process objective of community organisation. This means the "initiation and nourishment of a process in which all people of a community are involved in identifying and taking action in respect to their own problems. The emphasis is on cooperative and collaborative work. What is sought is increased motivation, responsibility and skill" (1967: 22).

What we suggest is that the introduction and implementation of IT into a social service organisation requires community organisation skills which, of course, are available to social workers. We are therefore not dealing with a process foreign to social work. This brings us to the question as to how do we use the outsider, the IT expert, in this process? The IT expert plays the same roles which the professional community organiser plays when attempting to bring about change in a community. The IT expert can be a *guide* helping the social service organisation finding the means to achieve its own goals through IT. The IT expert can be an *enabler* facilitating the IT process. The IT expert can be an *expert* providing information and direct advice regarding the IT process. The IT expert can even be a *therapist* too, diagnosing the social service agency's IT problems and through discussions with the staff providing answers regarding these issues.

The Tasks of the Information Technology Social Work Expert

If the outside consultant needs to use a range of community organisation and social work skills in facilitating the initial implementation of IT, then it will come as no surprise to learn that these very skills are also necessary for the "inside consultant": the person within the agency who works side-by-side with the external consultant. This IT social work expert will take over the task of spearheading implementation once the external consultant departs.

The "IT social worker expert" who is an integral part of the social service agency staff – an insider – does not work in a vacuum. The professional tools of social work are at hand. Dealing with the introduction of IT in a social work setting and the problems and stress which it creates has parallels with dealing with clients who have problems and are under stress as a result of change in their circumstances. Let's analyse in more detail the above tasks of the IT social worker.

There are five tasks which the "expert" has to undertake: (i) identify the impact of IT on the personnel of the social service organisation throughout the computerisation process; (ii) identify social problems which will come about as a result of this technological change; (iii) encourage the development of a social milieu within which these problems can be aired; (iv) stimulate a process which will enable the workers to deal with problems; (v) relate the social development of the workers to the technological development of the organisation by harmonising the two processes. We will deal with each of these in turn.

Identify the impact of IT on the workers of the social service organisation:

The identification of the impact of IT is a group process. Social workers should discuss openly their feelings regarding IT and the impact they feel it will make on their work. An impact may be positive or negative. Both alternatives should be presented with regard to: social workers personally, the social workers in their professional capacity and in relation to the social service organisation. For example:

Impact on	Positive	Negative
social service worker personally	feeling of empowerment	fear of administrative monitoring
social service worker professionally	management of the case	lose personal contact with the client
social service organisation	manage information system, decision support system	breakdown of informal organisation

The goal of the IT social worker at this stage is to balance the pros and cons of the impact of IT. This brings us to the next task of the IT social worker.

Identify social problems which will come about as a result of this technological change:

Negative impact should be defined within a problem format identifying the source of the problem and who it will affect. Social workers should prioritise problems, then discuss how they could deal with them. For example, in order to maximise personal contact with the client, they may decide not to enter information into the computer during an interview (even though it is very easy to do so with a user-friendly screen display) but instead to write brief notes during the interview and then enter the pertinent information after the client departs.

Encourage the development of a social milieu within which these problems can be aired:

Human judgement is an important factor in technological systems (McNown, 1986). The human aspect of IT programmes should be integrated into the technological system. Without good communication within an organisation you will have a computerised shambles (Dove, 1989). This is true not only on the technical level but also on the social level of the social service organisation. A social framework should exist within which social workers will be able to personalise the IT process. The informal communication network should be encouraged. It will personalise the IT process within a social milieu.

Stimulate a process which will enable the workers to deal with problems:

Within the framework created for following up the introduction of IT within the social service agency a process should be established which will enable social workers to deal with their problems relating to IT. This process should have both formal and informal channels. The formal channels could be used for discussing issues relevant to the organisation as a whole or to conditions of service (for example, the implications of computerised supervision upon relationships between various levels of staff). Informal channels can be used for discussing more personal issues. The social worker should be able to consult with colleagues in a comfortable, natural, informal setting. For example: as social service practice becomes more standardised within an IT setting (Gripton and Licker, 1986) informal case discussions between colleagues should be encouraged in order to maintain interpersonal collegiality.

Relate the social development of the workers to the technological development of the organisation:

This is the ultimate goal. The IT social work expert's mission is being fulfilled when social workers feel a harmony between their own professional role and values and the development of IT within the agency, for example in the implementation of a computerised case-monitoring system which integrates social work principles. Here the IT social worker should be a "bridge" between the social service staff and the IT staff alerting each side to issues of concern at each stage of the development process. In addition, the IT social worker can influence the IT process by indicating that a "social work expert" is as relevant as an IT expert to the introduction of IT into a social services agency.

Resource Requirements

Resource allocation in principle is so obvious that it ought not to need mentioning. One of the problems though, is that the hardware, always supposed to be the major cost, is only the tip of the resource iceberg. Much of the software, particularly upgrades, expansions and general maintenance, patchwork and trouble shooting, comprises an additional and often unexpected resource cost. But the really big cost is "human ware". The costs of training, retraining, consultation and general up-heaval are very great. Gandy and Tepperman (1990) report that software acqui-sition, staff training, expert consultation, and managerial time spent in thinking (and rethinking) about computerisation processes are far costlier than the hardware. They advise that no organisation should begin computerisation without having realistically assessed whether and how it can meet all the costs that will predict-ably (and unpredictably) arise.

Therein lies the rub. How does one predict the unpredictable? The answer is by learning from the experiences of others. Gandy and Tepperman tell us that the resource issue is closely correlated with planning. Agencies which plan ahead make more realistic judgements about costs. The issue of powerful sponsorship arises here too. The interest expressed by the backer of the implementation needs to be sustained: "Administrators and board members too often fail to sustain their in-terest in the technology after purchasing the hardware. As problem after problem arises, they prove unwilling to commit the resources needed to continue upgrad-ing the staff and system" (1990: 186).

So resources need to be linked to perseverance amongst implementers. It is not necessary to have a bottomless pit of money (though this would ease many of the problems); the crucial features are tenacity, vision and confidence in the future – all inextricably linked to either power or influence. For some large-scale and complex implementations in agencies without initially enthusiastic staff, all three of these attributes are needed.

Bronson et al. (1988) stress the problem of allocating staff resources both to undertake the computerisation process itself and to run parallel manual and com-puter systems during the running-in stage. Staff of the social service agency will need time to be trained in how to operate the computer, how to check the reports for errors, and how to correct problems in the data collection procedures. There is a need to run parallel systems during the implementation stage in case things go seriously wrong with the technology, and the manual system has to be kept running until it is certain that the computerised system is producing accurate re-ports. This duplication of effort can last up to a year, depending on the application.

There are various approaches to evaluating the resources required to implement IT in social service agencies. Clark (1988) reports that the costs associated with computerisation include researching the need, acquiring the materials, and training the workers. Glastonbury (1986) states that a considerable expenditure is needed for networking, training and servicing equipment. Hammer and Hile (1985) stress the resources needed to overcome staff resistance to automation and they also mention the hidden cost of producing proper documentation. Kreuger and Stretch (1990) list a wide range of initial acquisition costs and remind us that there are continuing organisational costs as well. These include: time required away from routine office activities, "down time" from equipment failure, regular maintenance, time to backup data, time retrieving lost data, and time spent on routine error checking. Schoech, Schkade and Mayers (1981) identify five factors which are needed for the development of an IT programme: time, money, effort, commitment and trust. These variables enable the agency to answer a key question in IT development. Does the agency have motivation, capacity and opportunity to proceed?

From the above it can be seen that the resource requirements for introducing IT in a social service agency can be broken down to two fundamental variables, i.e. *time* and *money*. The investment of these resources is not a once-off "deal"; rather it involves an investment over a considerable period of time. This begins with a feasibility study to obtain an overview of the existing system, identify the system strengths, weaknesses and user needs, prepare preliminary cost estimates and evaluate staff willingness to accept an automated system (Kucic, Sorensen and Hanbery, 1983). Once the decision is made to introduce IT the capital outlay for hardware and software quickly follows.

Looking at the IT process in its overall perspective this initial stage of resource investment may be the most pleasant. It is usually a period of excitement, with all the doubts and questions, as something new, modern and technological will be in the agency. What follows can be a great shock for management and social workers.

The greatest shock for both managers and social workers is the amount of staff time which is needed in order for IT to be successfully implemented (Bronson et al., 1988). Support and training is needed in four areas: the use of hardware, the use of software, the application of software for the agency's specific purposes and the translation of computer output into an information structure that other people can understand (de Graaf, 1987). Social workers often have a limited understanding of computer technology. This is because they have received little training in computer technology through the professional social work education curriculum, and social services agencies do not provide in-service training on computer technology (Pardeck, Umfress and Murphy, 1990).

Marsh, Omerod and Roberts (1986) describe a training process for introducing IT in a social service department. Everyone who would be ultimately involved in providing information or receiving information from the proposed system received training. This included 200 key members of staff: decentralised clerical and administrative support staff; professional, supervisory and management staff; and senior management. The initial exercise involved five half days basic familiarisation training for each member of staff. Members of staff who experienced difficulty were invited back for a further two half days prior to the next main phase of training. This second phase of three half days for each member of staff involved detailed briefing on the development of the mainframe project and first principles of its operation. The final phase, estimated at a further five half days per member of staff, is planned as part of the implementation exercise, and will involve detailed system operation. Further sessions on *ad hoc* enquiry facilities and specific microcomputer packages will follow in due course. In the middle of the overall programme, staff were given a half day's training literally the day before their equipment was installed, as a confidence booster.

Information Needs

Schoech (1979) reminds us that the easiest data to computerise may not be the most useful for decision-making. The mere existence of data is not a sufficient reason for collecting it (Simon, 1973). It becomes essential to establish a decision-making process to decide which data are necessary. Phillips, Dimsdale and Taft (1981) developed three criteria to help to decide on which information would be suitable to include in an information system:

1) Usability: How would the information be used, and what sorts of decisions might be based on it?
2) Appropriateness of computerisation: Could the information be handled without being part of the computer system?
3) Computer systems implication: What are the added costs to use the computer to handle the data?

One of the issues to be discussed in designing an information system is how much information do the different workers in the organisation need in order to carry out their tasks. The computer's appetite for input can create havoc with staff and administration. The walls of many social service organisations are filled with volumes of unused printout from those electronic devices (Sullivan, 1980). In describing the development of an automation project in the City of Antwerp van Hove reported that

> in the preliminary consultation rounds the social workers vied with each other in creativity to indicate information which in some special cases could be considered relevant. The systems analysts have converted these endless lists into a complex data system of over 150 screens eager to prove that anything can be handled by computers. The end result is an application where more than half the panels are never used (1989: 13).

But getting control of the *amount* of information required is only the first stage. The *accuracy* of information is also vital. Inaccurate input leads to a useless information system. An information system will highlight agency problems: "everything that is going wrong in the organisation can become a disaster after introducing computers" (de Graaf, 1987: 17). Automate an inadequate and poorly designed manual system and the results will be an inadequate and poorly designed computer system (Kucic, Sorensen and Hanbery, 1983). Therefore a social service agency *must* be able to define its tasks and information requirements in a highly professional social service manner before it can even *begin* to computerise.

Is more data useful? Janson (1980) reports that an increase in the number of reports can obscure rather than illuminate. Computers provide vast quantities of data for decision-makers, often overloading them with too much, too quickly (Vogel, 1985). In order to avoid such an over-production of information it becomes important that the reasons and methods for collecting each piece of data should be specified. On the other hand, Bronson et al. (1988) claim that in most agencies informational needs grow after implementing a computerised information system. Therefore it is necessary to start slowly, carefully and accurately and then to expand informations systems gradually, preferably in a modular fashion.

This is particularly important when generating reports for monitoring or statistical purposes. It is very easy to produce a large number of these on a regular basis. There are two dangers here. The first is the production of a plethora of useless information, and the second of the non-production of information which is required. Inefficient staff involvement can bring about a situation where reports needed by the social worker are found to be missing from the menu of the IT programme ("I didn't think of it"). This situation leads to demoralisation on the part of the staff and under-use of a power instrument in the decision-making process. On the other hand, over-reporting can bring about confusion ("What do I need all this data for?"). Therefore, the design of the report-generating programme should be closely related to staff information needs. Velasquez and Lynch (1981) warn us not to collect data and produce reports unless their use can be justified. "Interesting to know" items should be discarded. On the opposite end of the scale in order to think of everything that is needed for a report generator the following questions should be asked (Kucic, Sorensen and Hanbery, 1983).

• What are the user's information needs?
• What reports are to be generated?
• When are the reports to be produced?

Conclusions

The most important factors in successfully implementing IT in the social services can be summarised under two heads: organisational and human. The most crucial organisational factors relate to time, money and organisational resilience and readiness to computerise. A crucial factor in the readiness of the organisation to computerise relates to the effectiveness of structures and channels for communicating, consulting and participating in decision-making. And it is human factors which are crucial to these channels. Continuous and genuine involvement of staff at all levels, coupled with sensitivity to their potential worries is a *sine qua non* of effective implementation.

Two roles are pivotal to successful implementation. The first is that of sponsor: a person with power in the organisation, with the enthusiasm and stamina to overcome the serious problems which always accompany institutional change. The second is the inside consultant – the "Information Technology Social Worker" who will smooth over the difficulties of implementation and transition, and will ensure that the IT system keeps in step with changes in the organisation's structure.

CHAPTER 7

IT in Action in the Social Services

Here we come to the culmination of the book's purpose: IT up and running in social work agencies, doing the job it was intended for – enhancing social work. We look first at a range of applications in the areas of social work information, assessment and supervision systems. Then we review some well-established innovations in the use of decision support systems. Fittingly for a book on innovations, we end with an exploration of some experiments at the cutting edge of technological developments in the field of expert systems.

Social Work Information, Assessment and Supervision Systems

There are a whole host of straightforward, unpretentious, low cost and useful computer applications which were designed to be used by social workers in their daily practice (Phillips, 1987). It is also possible to create an effective customised package using sophisticated off-the-shelf applications. For example Reinoehl, Brown and Iroff (1990) developed computer assisted life reviews using an ideas processor combined with a word processor and a graphics package. Even when creating a completely new package it is not necessary to develop a vast all-encompassing computer database – a relatively simple system can be of major benefit to social workers so long as it is properly conceptualised. We commence our review with exactly such a system.

KnoW – a Knowledge Workstation

A diary and a filing cabinet full of case records is the only information system available to many social workers – and this is not necessarily a bad thing. Many social workers have suffered under the implementation of badly designed and used unfriendly management-initiated information systems. Monnickendam and Yaniv's (1989) starting point is that it is better not to have a computerised system than to have a bad one. They pose the question: why should social workers alter their way of practising just to fit in to the requirements of a system whose purpose is to help them in their daily work? They criticise the design of many of the existing management-oriented systems where a higher priority is given to effective data storage manipulation than to effective use by social workers and they claim that this leads to the information systems being rigid, compartmentalised and cumbersome to use. More to the point, these systems are designed *inappropriately* for effective use by social workers:

> We are dealing with situations where the practitioner usually browses through the file, directed often by associative thinking. Their aim is not to extract data but to learn about their clients. The learning process utilises associative and logical thinking, combining data from multiple types and sources, and jumps between different levels of abstraction. Thus, the conceptual base of a software program that should truly serve the practitioner and not vice versa has to be much more open ... An information system should assist its user to utilise his or her knowledge to the utmost. In order to design an information system it is not sufficient to know *what* information is used and required but also *how* information is used and manipulated and what functions it has to support. It is impossible to separate the "what" and the "how" of an information system (Monnickendam and Yaniv, 1989: 3-4).

The goal they set themselves was to create a system aimed at supporting the social work practitioner's normal method of functioning in a natural way. In order to achieve this they studied case records and interviewed and observed social workers. They discerned the following pattern of information use:

- recurrent determination of relevant information;
- data fusion as a means of creating new information;
- ongoing case evaluation;
- understanding the rationale for past decisions and evaluations;
- consideration of conditions for intervention;
- juxtaposing multiple levels of abstraction;
- interdisciplinary exchange of information.

From this they developed the KnoW environment which consists of four core components:

1) data items or knowledge resources;
2) tasks to be performed;
3) links between and among knowledge resources and tasks;
4) orientation devices like maps to navigate among knowledge resources and tasks.

KnoW was initially devised for use in a child development centre where children were evaluated on a range of factors. This was performed on the computer by a technique they called "bar(r)ing" – meaning to rate on a bar and to lay bare.

The bar can be moved up and down using the mouse and the labels can be changed to suit the client's circumstances. The rationale of bar(r)ing is that social workers do make judgements about progress and activity but are not normally able to provide precise measures so a relational scale is both appropriate and unproblematic: "Bar(r)ing is a visual representation of a perceived situation relative to a former situation, in most cases, or a known standard. A 'justification window' is also provided. The bargraphs are presented and compared at case conferences. They can also be converted into time series graphs which again can be linked with the 'justifications'" (Monnickendam and Yaniv, 1989: 12).

Map and compass icons are provided to help social workers to navigate through the information environment. This enables them to browse through the data un-hampered by way the database is structured. A pre-planned route is provided for inexperienced users. Social workers experienced in using KnoW normally browse through the system in the same way they would through manual case notes, adapt-ing their approach to the individual circumstances of each case:

> Due to the capacity for navigation and the presence of links, adaptation of the level of abstraction to the occasion at hand is easy. The combined display of different knowledge resources lets the practitioner consider multiple levels of abstraction in unison and fuse new knowledge (Monnickendam and Yaniv, 1989: 18).

So here we have a practitioner-friendly up-and-running social work information system. By one of the sad ironies of IT funding in the social services this system has not been further developed or translated (it was programmed for use in the Hebrew language). Even though it has demonstrated its use to *practitioners* there has been little support from *managers* who do not directly benefit from it – effec-tive social work does not necessarily save money.

Client Assessment Systems

A safer way to get a system supported and sponsored is to start off with a well-established *manual* system and then computerise it.

More has probably been written on client assessment than on any other area of computerisation in the social services. Much of the writing has been aimed spe-cifically at clinical psychologists but there is an impressive literature too on as-sessment of clients in social work *per se* (Nurius, 1990b). Unfortunately, much of the literature suffers from the often combined effects of two *bêtes noires* which we have met before – computer enthusiasts and ruthless salespeople. The desire of enthusiasts to itemise, codify and analyse is salutary if it relates to carefully thought-through assessment strategies but it needs to be kept in check if it is not to outrun its usefulness. And unfortunately the computer gives the ideal opportunity for enthusiasts to engage in proliferating schedules and questionnaires at a great rate. When this is coupled with the desire to make profits by marketing assessment programmes for profit then the outcome verges on a pseudo-psychometric deluge.

The quality and utility of many of these offerings are low. We will concentrate our attention instead on the highly respected, extensively documented and rigourously validated system developed over many years, and initially for manual administration, by William Hudson – the Clinical Assessment System (CAS).

The CAS (Nurius and Hudson, 1988) starts with a computerised version of an intake questionnaire or of an initial social history. The user can then access any of 20 inbuilt clinical measures, several clinical inventories and Likert-type scales. The CAS incorporates progress monitoring and has extensive file modification and statistical facilities. Once the social history or questionnaire information has been collected, the programme will prepare a report which can be printed or reviewed on the screen. In addition there is a "scale design" facility which enables an unlimited number of additional instruments to be incorporated into the package and provides standardised measures and score interpretations.

The production of a barrage of scores on clinical assessments and inventories can be disconcerting for the inexperienced user, even though the computer does generate explanations and graphical interpretations of each score which is produced. The authors claim that the single most powerful feature of the programme consists of its ability to save client scores obtained from virtually any assessment scale and then present them in graphic form for use by the client and the worker. They tell us that this leads to greater client participation in the planning, monitoring and evaluation of treatment, and for incorporating client perspectives into case conferences, supervision, and programme or unit evaluation (Nurius and Hudson, 1989: 27-29).

In a later paper, though, Nurius does qualify the unbridled optimism of her earlier work with Hudson:

> At this point in time, both the problems and the promises of computer-assisted assessment are significant. By and large, the view that the sound advantages outweigh the sound criticisms, and that the computer offers a unique complementary (rather than supplanting) role is a representative and well supported perspective. One of the most pressing areas of need is a more systematic and thorough evaluation of computerised tools. ... much more extensive and refined validation research is called for as is creative research focused on more fully utilising the computer's capacities, and on the relation of the computer to other aspects of clients' and the practitioners' thoughts, feelings and actions (Nurius, 1990).

Here she identifies the crucial dilemma in clinical testing. It is much easier to administer these tests than to know what to do with their results. Testing can be useful for diagnostic purposes, but it needs to be precisely focused in order to be of much use in intervention, treatment or therapy. In other words the social worker needs to have a holistic *intervention strategy* of which clinical assessment is a part.

Supervision

Hudson used an eclectic approach to clinical assessment in designing the CAS; he produced his own scales but also provided an environment where users could create their own measures and bolt them on to the package. Cnaan (1988b) took a radically different stance in his experiment in using computers to assist in social work supervision. Cnaan's approach was integrative and holistic in substance and is based on the methodology of knowledge engineering. He developed a two-stage model for creating a computerised supervision package. Stage 1 involves selection of relevant variables and stage 2 the incorporation of supervisor's comments. At first sight this does not appear to be too difficult a task but it was beset by problems. After four years of work the agency was still struggling to get it sorted out. The key criteria for inclusion of variables included: relevance to clinical practice; the ideology, regulations and mode of service delivery of the agency; clear, measurable, mutually exclusive items; relevance of issue to supervisors; and ability of social workers to gather relevant data in the normal course of their work.

In the second stage the supervisors had to agree upon the meaning of possible answers. They had to identify what specific case data meant for practice; that is, how the information would be used in routine supervision. This is where the knowledge engineering came in, via the process of using knowledge and experience to identify clinical meanings relevant to practice. Given the problems involved in designing even the most straightforward expert system, this seems an extraordinarily ambitious goal.

In each case the supervisor had to undertake three major tasks: first, identify the most important questions both therapeutically and administratively; secondly, summarise the *meaning* of the data – i.e. how a supervisory session would be conducted on its basis; and thirdly, install the "supervisory knowledge module" (SKM) in the computer and determine what categories would generate a given SKM printout. The notion of a SKM is ambitious. The general idea is that clinical supervisory knowledge is summarised in a brief essay which is stored in the computer memory. Supervisory material printouts which suggest interpretations and/or course of action are then generated in relation to individual cases on the basis of clinically relevant categories triggered by keywords in the client and supervisory databases. There are similarities with expert systems in that the computerised supervisory summaries suggest possible actions. But there is a major difference: "unlike expert systems, these summaries have no certainty factors, and the final decisions rest with the line workers" (Cnaan, 1988b: 129).

As an example, he tells us that there are two supervisors in Israel with a good knowledge of fraud probation cases who have done extensive knowledge engineering on this issue. They identified four groups which respond to different intervention strategies.

> This agglomeration of knowledge, which had been summarised into two typed pages, was stored in the computer. Thereafter, whenever a probation officer entered 'fraudulence' as a cause of referral by the court for a client, the computer would generate a SKM printout about personality types as well as suggested interventions. The worker who receives the printout is also cautioned that his/her client may be an exception to the basic personality types. The worker is also given the names of the two supervisors in the service who are experts in the field. She/he is advised to consult these experts if she/he finds the client is an exceptional case (Cnaan, 1988b: 131).

The overall goal is to relieve supervisors of routine administration and educational duties and allow them to concentrate on "the more challenging, creative and stimulating aspects of their work" (p. 133). However, Cnaan forecasts that it will take at least a decade to evaluate the innovation.

In similar vein it is worth recalling the cautionary conclusions reached by Benbenishty and Ben-Zaken (1988) in their discussion of a computer-aided monitoring of social work intervention. They remind us that the ultimate reason for the design and operation of clinical information systems is to improve practice in order to provide better help for clients, but they themselves do not expect to be in a position to ask the question in an empirical study for years to come. They also gloomily tell us that they strongly believe a cost-benefit analysis would indicate that the costs outweigh the direct benefits attained in their project and they finish by saying "Perhaps researchers are getting carried away by the technology" (Benbenishty and Ben-Zaken, 1988: 9).

Decision Support Systems

Decision Support Systems (DSS) have a well established history in the annals of computer science. They have been tried and tested in a wide variety of commercial, industrial and public service settings and they can be demonstrated to be useful when dealing with specific, quantifiable problems which are amenable to the statistical logic of linear regression.

Over a decade ago Schoech and Schkade first introduced the possibility of using DSS in social work. They described a DSS as a computer-based data processing application designed to assist professionals in making complex decisions: "A DSS can be visualised as multiple computerised data-bases connected and organised to help the decision-maker retrieve, manage and display information relevant to the decision at hand" (Schoech and Schkade, 1980b: 567). They did not create a precise typology of the principles of a DSS but their starting point was to look at the needs of a practising social worker. They spelled out what they considered to be the essence of a social work DSS as follows:

1) Recall of factual data, key activities and events of similar cases as well as some indication of whether the case was successfully handled.
2) Processing the information into an organised format that is readily usable.
3) Capacity to instantaneously analyse and synthesize the information from similar cases (using raw data, summary data or trend data, to answer "what if" types of questions and to use that information in making predictions about the present case).
4) Knowledge of agency rules and procedures, and how they affect the present case.
5) Assistance in making the most appropriate decision by combining factual data, professional experience, and intuitive judgement with the information from similar cases (ibid.).

By the mid 1980s the term "decision support system" was being used with more precision. Vogel (1985) characterised DSS as "interactive computer-based systems that help decision makers utilise data and models to solve unstructured problems" and he created a rigorous taxonomy of the purposes which DSS have to fulfil. They:

1) are intended to be supportive to decision-makers, not to replace them;
2) are aimed at less well structured problems which tend to lack complete specification;
3) seek to combine the use of models and analytic techniques with more customary data access and retrieval functions;
4) are interactive and "friendly" to the decision-maker, and thus seek to be supportive to users who are not "computer people";
5) are intentionally flexible in order to be able to adapt to changes in the organisation's environment and to the individual needs of the decision-maker;
6) often involve the use of large databases whose structure and content may be overwhelming to the decision-maker in the absence of supportive tools (Vogel, 1985: 68).

Vogel identifies three problems which need to be confronted before the productive use of sophisticated DSS is likely to occur.

Problem 1: Describing the actual decision-making processes that take place in the social services

He claims that at present there is too little information describing decisions and decision-making processes in the social services to offer more than just a general sense of direction about where research should be heading in this area. He is also very critical of Schoech and Schkade (1980b). He claims that while their vision of a social work DSS represents interesting speculation of what a social services DSS *might* be, it leaves unanswered a number of significant questions about the structure of decisions caseworkers make:

> They list a series of choices available to a direct services worker who is accessing the DSS in search of support. These choices involve, for example, a *summary narrative* of *similar cases* that were *resolved successfully*, or alternatively, the identification of *key activities* that were judged to have been handled successfully. The underlined words and phrases would need to be defined clearly during the process of DSS development, *before* the DSS could be used productively by the casework staff. This is a very difficult challenge, given our current state of knowledge about casework intervention. In addition, Schoech and Schkade's DSS appears to be based on a model of decision-making behaviour such as might currently be observed *in the absence of* a DSS. Thus it does not anticipate likely changes in the decision making process itself *as a result of* DSS development (Vogel, 1985: 76, emphasis in original).

He cites studies which are starting to make progress in describing decision-making and which are taking the first steps in social services decision structure and process. His aims are very ambitious. Instead of just supporting and copying *existing* decision-making processes, he wants to find out how DSS can *alter* and *improve upon* these processes: "since the creative use of computer support has the potential to shift existing decision making patterns to what we hope will be more effective approaches" (ibid.).

He is jumping the gun here and seems to be in danger of contradicting his first principle, namely that DSS are intended to support, not replace, decision-makers. He is in effect prematurely embracing the notion of artificial intelligence – of some sort of quantum leap into a brave new world of innovative and qualitatively different forms of machine-led decision-making. It is, of course, true that effective DSS will lead to changes in decision-making, but these changes will be incremental and will operate via a process of enhancing rather than transcending human thinking. We will see just how this can happen when we investigate Shapira's (1990) probation DSS later in this chapter.

Problem 2: Increasing our understanding of what enhances effective social services decision-making.

Here Vogel whets our appetite, but gives us no indication of how a DSS might solve this problem. He rephrases the question as follows: "What decisions lead to interventions and programmes that make a difference in terms of the objectives sought?" His answer is in terms of the differences between efficiency and effectiveness. He reminds us that computers have often increased efficiency by mechanising repetitive manual data processing activities but he claims that DSS can increase effectiveness, even at a cost of reducing efficiency: "DSS attempts to address issues of effectiveness explicitly, and in some applications, will accept a less efficient use of resources in order to realise greater effectiveness" (Vogel, 1985: 77). Unfortunately he gives us no indication whatsoever of how this can be done within the confines of even his own definition of a DSS. The only clues we have from his taxonomy are that DSS use large databases and that they use models and analytical techniques. One is left with the suspicion that he has let his imagination run riot to the extent that his vision of DSS dramatically transcends that of even the most ambitious expert system. Fortunately he does come back down to Earth before leaving this issue and he reminds himself of our extremely limited knowledge of cause and effect in social work and of the complexities of evaluating the results of intervention. This leads him to the conclusion that there is much to be learned in this important area.

Problem 3: Increasing our use of data in social services decision-making.

He gets on to much safer ground here. His comments are more prosaic but also more useful:

> In the human services generally, decisions and decision making processes are often not 'data based'. Decisions which stem from intuitive models, or indeterminate knowledge bases, often rely more on experience, judgement, attitudes and predispositions than on data. But the promise of computers and DSS – even in the human services – are closely linked to the ability to use *data* more effectively in making decisions. There are of course a number of reasons why decision makers do not use data – training and background, unreliable data collection procedures, lack of confidence in the data that are collected, and a lack of cognitive decision making models which require data (Vogel, 1985: 77-78).

This is salutary advice, and is particularly relevant in deciding whether or not to adopt a DSS. If decisions are based on experience and judgement rather than on data then it is not advisable to institute a DSS. These sorts of decisions, if they are amenable to computerisation at all, are more suited to expert systems. The strength of DSS is their ability to cope with finite and relatively well-defined problems as opposed to infinite and ill-defined problems.

Decision Support Systems in Action: Two Case-Studies

These two case-studies were chosen to highlight the strengths and weaknesses of decision support systems. In the first, an ambitious attempt to apply DSS methodology to family therapy came face to face with all three of Vogel's problems. In practical terms the quality and use of data was a major issue, but the biggest conceptual problem was a lack of matching between the decision-making processes of family therapists and the mathematical model underlying decision support systems.

In the second example, probation officers' court reports, a decision support system demonstrates its worth. Here the criteria for decision-making are based on equity, the data used is specific and consistent from case to case, and the process of decision-making by probation officers is compatible with the underlying logic of decision support systems.

1: Family Therapy

Gripton, Licker and de Groot (1988) approached the subject from a perspective similar to that of Vogel. They introduced a wide-ranging DSS in a family therapy setting. While claiming that the development of professional support systems is potentially the most rewarding aspect of new technology in the social services they nevertheless kept their feet solidly on the ground by pointing out that DSS are extremely costly and time-consuming in an area as imprecise and (in decision-making terms) nebulous as social work intervention.

The implementation of their DSS did not run smoothly. This may be partly because they took an uncompromising stance on the introduction of new technology: they insisted that the effective introduction of new technology required substantial changes in social worker practice. For example, they claimed that effective computerisation of clinical records "requires social workers to make fundamental shifts in how they think about cases, observe clients and record clinical events" (Gripton et al., 1988: 78).

They created the DSS framework by first investigating the information requirements of family therapists. They then analysed how therapists made clinical decisions by observing and recording group supervision sessions and interviewing individual therapists about their method of working. The final outcome was an integrated software package centred upon a clinical database programme which comprised: client descriptions; assessment file; intervention file, and evaluation file. Family map programmes, resource programmes and an information system all fed into the package, as did the Personal Consulting Decision Support System (PCDSS). The PCDSS is designed to simulate the way that human consultants or supervisors give advice. Its method, though, is somewhat mechanistic. It is based upon "similarity functions" in that it refers to other families which have some similar attributes to the one under discussion, and it gives the success rates for different therapy types in these previous cases. The method is explained in detail in the text and is worth studying.

The authors do not give an evaluation of the package but they do say that three important constraints need to be overcome if its potential is to be fully realised. First, we are told that the characteristics of the clinical data and the way they are used by social workers must be substantially modified. They say that this task is one not likely to be taken on board by social workers without convincing demonstration of the practice gains that will be forthcoming, but it is possible that the uncompromising nature of their initial approach may have alienated the workers who were implementing the system.

The second problem lies in the quality of social work measurement data, not only in terms of inputs, but of outputs also – measures of actual practice effectiveness. This mirrors Vogel's plaintive comments about effectiveness of social work. It appears that they were too ambitious in their expectations of the possibilities of meaningfully quantifying inputs and outcomes in social work.

Thirdly, and by far the most problematic: "the underlying logic of PCDSS applications is a linear model of cause and effect, whereas popular theories of family therapy are based upon cybernetic models" (Gripton et al., 1988: 85). This total mismatch in the structure and process of reasoning appears to be a fundamental barrier to the use of the present generation of DSS in modelling the more complex and holistic aspects of social work decision-making. This is a crucial insight. It is absolutely vital to match the nature of the problem-solving methodology to the nature of the problem itself.

The strength of their work lies not in the success of their DSS implementation – for it does not appear to have been successful – but in the insight they have gained and transmitted about the problems which have to be overcome in attempting to use IT meaningfully in the social services. After their sobering description of DSS in action, the authors move on to a wide-ranging and excellent discussion of general administrative and human relations issues in the introduction of computers to clinical practice. They give a perceptive overview of the possible good, bad and indifferent consequences of computerisation. Along the way they explore different possible responses of social workers to new technology and they produce a flow chart which should be framed and placed on the office wall of everyone who wants to introduce computers into social work settings. The algorithm deals with the steps necessary in planning a computerised system and highlights basic issues of interest, commitment, resources and practicality. It does not ignore the different needs of managers and practitioners. Also – a sobering reminder of reality – it has an awful lot of arrows which point to the box entitled *"Abandon Computerisation Plan"*.

2: The Jerusalem Probation Service

This section draws heavily upon Shapira (1990) and Shapira and Levi (1990).

This second case-study tells a happier story where the computerisation plan did not have to be abandoned. Here the decision support system grew from strength to strength and became fully embedded within the Israel Probation Service. Its strength lies in its simplicity. It supports one very specific decision – the recommendation made to the court by a Probation Officer about a juvenile found guilty of an indictable offence. This decision is precise and it is bounded, there are only 15 possible alternatives. It is made on the basis of limited information gathered from one or two interviews with the offender which are structured around the completion of a social enquiry report. It is intended to be a fair, equitable and professional decision, so it should stand the test of comparison with similar cases. And it is of major significance to the life chances and quality of life of the offender because the courts take this "disposal recommendation" into careful consideration when sentencing offenders.

Before the development of the DSS, concern was raised about the extent to which Probation Officers' decisions were fair, equitable and reliable. Shapira (1981) undertook an investigation of 1,284 disposal recommendations and came to two conclusions. First, she demonstrated that it was appropriate to use linear regression equations (and therefore decision support systems) to model Probation Officers' recommendations. She was able to derive a set of rules from the limited information in the case files which reproduced about half the variance in disposal recommendations. This gave her DSS a large head start on that of Gripton et al. (1988) in the first case-study, who were never confident that linear regression was an adequate technique for modelling the decisions of family therapists. Secondly, she found that there was room for considerable improvement in consistency and explicitness in their decision-making. Of course, a proportion of the apparent discrepancy can be attributed to consistent but unrecorded (and perhaps unrecordable) factors accruing to subtle nuances of professional judgement. But it is equally true that some was due to bias, error and inconsistency of judgement. The DSS was created in order to minimise these unwanted causes of variance.

Shapira's DSS did not encounter the problems of mismatch between social work logic and DSS logic which beset the professional support system in our first example. She achieved this by building the system entirely on the past decisions of the Probation Officers themselves and by avoiding the temptation of incorporating any prescriptive notions of what would be the "right" decisions. So the system is normative – it distils and reflects the norms of the workers.

The purpose of the DSS in the Youth Probation Service is to help Probation Officers to maintain a fair balance between two sometimes conflicting factors. The first is the freedom to exercise professional discretion in considering the distinctive aspects of an individual case. The second, on the other hand, is the requirement of explicitness, visibility, predictability, and consistency of decision-making procedures which is necessary for the provision of equitable and reliable recommendations in the assignment of juvenile offenders

The system does not aim at replacing Probation Officers and their professional judgement, nor to provide rigid rules for optimal solutions. It attempts to correct situations in which a great deal of uncontrolled discretion in the hands of field level personnel may result in arbitrary, inconsistent and inequitable decisions which affect vital interests of a very vulnerable population. The system's aim is to develop, in a gradual and evolutionary way, policy rules which are all derived from the previous actions of Probation Officers so they do not necessarily represent the *best* decisions but they do represent in effect the *collective practice wisdom* of the Probation Service.

The DSS in Action

The system proceeds through the following steps:

1) The Probation Officer enters the information about the youngster in a standard-ised, precoded form by conducting a question-answer dialogue with the com-puter. At the end of each section (e.g. "family background") the programme que-ries the Probation Officer about possible omissions and errors and permits in-sertion of additional material. In addition, the programme contains a "query facility" (in the form of a window display), which enables the Probation Officer to ask for additional knowledge stored in the data file. This enables information on some of the judgemental variables to be encoded in a uniform way.

2) Once all the information has been recorded the programme prompts the Proba-tion Officer to enter a disposition recommendation for the youngster from the 15 possible options provided by law.

3) The programme then computes and displays the disposition assignment gener-ated for that particular youngster by applying the rules embedded in the model in the information entered by the Probation Officer. The computer shows the Probation Officer what the disposition would have been for a youngster of like description if it had been made on the basis of the rules generated from all pre-vious cases which had been logged. Probation Officers are instructed to treat the rule-generated assignments not as commands but as additional significant information that may help guide the exercise of their discretion.

4) Next, the programme computes and displays in numerical values the disparity between the disposition selected by the Probation Officer and that generated by the model.

5) The programme continues by questioning the Probation Officer about his or her response to the model-generated decision. When there is a disparity between the Probation Officer's recommendation and that of the model, the Probation Officer is given the choice of which recommendation to adopt and is asked to enter the grounds for his or her preference. Typically, substantive reasons given for choosing to adhere to one's own decision are linked with information re-garding the particular youngster which is not included in the present model, or with the existence of an atypical situation or contingencies that contribute to the uniqueness of a particular case.

The deviations and Probation Officer's comments are stored in the database and are periodically analysed to discover valid new cues and substitute strong cues for the weak ones, thereby refining and improving the initial model.

6) Finally, the programme permits entering information on the court's decision regarding the case at a later date.

It can be seen that the professional experts, in this case the Youth Probation Officers, maintain their independence in making individual decisions and, in doing so, enhance the knowledge base of the decision support system. Moreover, many of the informational items involved subjective evaluations of individual youngsters and their families, and their coding ("measurement") can only be supplied by the Probation Officers in their capacity as professionals.

The Impact of the Decision Support System

Perhaps the most impressive feature of the implementation of the DSS is the ease with which it was incorporated into daily professional practice. What began as hesitant attempts by Probation Officers to enter information from written records and to get the computer's suggestions of dispositions has now become routine procedure. Probation Officers now enter all their cases into the computer, record their recommendations and enter their comments when there is a difference between their recommendation and what the computerised rules predict. When the DSS was put into full operation in 1986, approximately 51% of the variance in Probation Officer disposition recommendations were explained by variance in characteristics of the youngsters. By 1990, this figure was up to 71%.

Providing Probation Officers with information from the database on their actual decision behaviour has generated critical self-examination and involved Probation Officers in resolving ambiguities, controversies and inconsistencies in existing practice. This has led to them formalising additional rules consistent with their professional knowledge and requirements of equity, as well as to adding new facilities to the DSS system.

The DSS is also remarkably popular with practitioners. Shapira and Levi undertook a user satisfaction study in 1990 on the Probation Officers in Tel Aviv and Jerusalem. The response was highly positive. Probation Officers like the DSS because it provides advice, guidance and assistance but does not deprofessionalise them by imposing its judgements. They still retain the discretion to make their own disposal recommendations and they feel that the DSS does not impinge upon their professional judgement. Closely related to the desire to protect their professional authority is their unanimous expression of satisfaction from being able to follow up their own decisions with the help of the computer's record. Similarly the Probation Officers appreciate the institutionalised effort to continuously adjust the DSS through the work of a steering committee.

Workers did not express any fear of dehumanisation or growth of technocratic nature of the service as a result of the DSS introduction. They were generally positive to the notion that use of the DSS enhanced equity. The authors noted that a longer experience with DSS leads to a greater appreciation of its impact on fairness and equity in decision-making. They found evidence that the connection between utilisation of similar information in each case and the working of the system is well understood by the Probation Officers: "The prevailing majority of Probation Officers admit that when such disparity occurs and is displayed on the computer's screen, it stimulates them to give a second thought to their own recommendations. Nevertheless, they assert that these disparities do not undermine their confidence in their judgement or feel less sure of the conclusions reached by them" (Shapira and Levi, 1990: 20). Most Probation Officers also felt that there was no significant discrepancy between their own decisions and those generated by the DSS. This perception enhances the supportiveness they feel they get from the DSS and undoubtedly increases their confidence in its use.

The authors' conclusions about the Probation Officers' responses to the DSS are highly positive: "Finally, the strongest testimony to the effect that Probation Officers' attitude to the DSS tends to be a positive one, is provided by their expressed willingness to recommend introduction of the DSS to other social services" (Shapira and Levi, 1990: 26).

Shapira and Levi were less enthusiastic, though, about the response of management. One of the original purposes of the DSS was to enhance management monitoring and supervision of the work of Probation Officers. But it soon became clear that this was not happening, as Shapira and Levi ruefully note

> The designers of the system feel quite disappointed with the little, if any, imprint that the DSS made on the patterns and control and supervision over the decision-practice. ... Since the outputs available from DSS provide upon request, quite a detailed record of decision-behaviour of the officers individually and collectively, the little effect that they exercise upon Probation Officers' awareness most probably means that this information is not being utilised in supervisor-officer relationship, neither is it being used by the management for evaluation of service performance and for introduction of corrective procedure. This warrants serious attention, since it indicates that one of the most important functions of a DSS is being missed. The DSS was designed to act as a monitoring device which aims at controlling and correcting the decision-making of the Probation Officers and improving service policy (ibid.).

Implications for the Future

This DSS was in one sense an outstanding and unqualified success – the Probation Officers found it immensely useful in their day-to-day work and in their professional development. In other words *they felt it enabled them to do a better job*. But in another sense it was a damp squib. It did not impinge at all on the organisation and management of the Probation Service (except at an individual case-by-case level). Apparently it was not even used in professional or managerial supervision sessions with workers – which is what it was specifically designed to do.

Now, this "failure" is not necessarily a bad thing. The DSS is up and running and is accepted by the workers. This is a firm basis upon which to build. There ought not be too many problems in gradually introducing the DSS into professional supervision and then into managerial monitoring. It is easier to develop staff monitoring and appraisal from a position of confidence in the monitoring system than to introduce both simultaneously.

The major significance of the approach used by Shapira is that it is grounded in practice wisdom built up from analysis of the work previously done by Probation Officers and does not try to impose an external or "objective" wisdom.

It looks hopeful that this is not just an isolated example. Pruger informs us about a decision support system which moves into the area of innovation. The system was implemented in three county welfare departments in the San Francisco Bay area of California. It was used to help workers to assess client eligibility for the welfare department's In Home Supportive Services. One of the main problems previously was to ensure equity in service across the case load. In an equitable service all of the variance in service awards should be explained by differences in client characteristics, given that eligibility is clearly based upon clients' financial needs and physical impairment: "When the project began, 60% of the variance in service awards was explained by the variance in client characteristics. When the project ended, the figure was between 85% and 90%. Thus the 120 workers in the three demonstration counties, many of whom never saw or spoke to each other, came to follow the same rules and apply them consistently. The project accomplished this while it eliminated many top-down rules and guidelines, and reduced the detailed and onerous hierarchical supervision" (Pruger, 1986: 221).

This is an interesting example of what looks like a positive sum game in that the management of the organisation achieved one of its aims of increasing equity and standardising services while the social workers were released from supervision which they had found oppressive. They were also involved in developing and refining the system so they "owned" it and were able actively to develop the assessment system using their own professional expertise.

His overall conclusion, though, was less optimistic than Shapira's: "The IHSS [In Home Supportive Services] experience left us with the overall conclusion that properly implemented DSS can substantially increase the amount of rational decision-making in social service organisations ... However, we found that it is extraordinarily difficult to realise this potential, and that raises the issue of whether or not the effort involved is worthwhile" (p. 223). From Shapira's evidence it looks like it certainly may be.

Expert Systems

We have seen that DSS work best in specific, well-defined domains amenable to regression analysis and model-building using a limited range of variables. However, much of the decision-making in the social services lies in non-specific, ill-defined domains which are not amenable to the relatively straightforward world of regression analysis but are subject to the influence of apparently limitless variables

Before getting to grips with the nature of expert systems it is important to understand what they are not. The phrase "expert system" seems to engender a response resembling mild hysteria amongst some of the more excitable social service academics. For example Murphy and Pardeck (in Pardeck and Murphy, 1990) tell us "Because expert systems are supposed to act like human experts, the mind and a computer are presumed to be alike" and "the belief that computers mimic the functions of the mind makes sense only if human cognition and computerisation are similar". We are then regaled with several key assumptions about "biological, psychological, epistemological and even ontological assumptions" (Murphy and Pardeck, 1990c: 76). This formulation misconstrues the basis of the nature of expert systems – the mind and a computer are most emphatically *not* supposed to be alike. Similarly the expert system makes no pretence at making better decisions than the human social work expert, as its reliability is measured according to the criteria of how often it comes to the same answer as the human expert.

Definitions

Schoech, Jennings, Schkade and Hooper-Russell give the following definition:

> Expert systems are software programs which apply inference mechanisms to knowledge bases to extract decisions. Expert systems apply large stores of domain specific knowledge to a given set of facts to arrive at a solution at skill levels comparable with the human experts they mimic. Developers of expert systems utilise the computer to rapidly process masses of non-numeric symbols as well as using it as a large powerful number-crunching machine which manipulates quantities (Schoech et al., 1985: 88).

This seems very plausible, but there is not much substance behind all the big words. Perhaps the most straightforward definition is the one given by Goodman, Gingerich and de Shazer: "An expert system in essence is a computer programme which embodies the expertise of a human expert in order to consult on a specific problem" (1989: 53). This has the advantage of being brief and clear, but in itself is still not very informative. Fortunately, they do go on and give us some guidelines They report that the first, and possibly most difficult step in developing an expert system is to select a suitable problem. It must be one for which genuine experts exist, and it must be neither too difficult to make the task impossible nor too easy to make it unnecessary:

> As a general rule, the problem should be one that requires a human expert an hour or two to solve. The problem should be worthwhile in the sense that development of an expert system will make scarce expertise more widely available, or improve the quality of service provided. Finally, the problem must be one that is appropriate for the technology. It should be one that is best solved by heuristics or rules of thumb rather than a conventional algorithm or mathematical formula (Goodman et al., 1989: 56-57).

It is the notion of the rule of thumb which is both the strength and the Achilles Heel of expert systems. Its strength is that it provides a means of translating a process which feels intuitive to the expert. A series of rules strung together in a logical or probabilistic way often provides the most successful computer approximation of a human expert's decision-making. But the problem lies in getting the experts to unlock in their own minds the processes which they actually follow when making decisions and to describe them accurately and completely in terms which are sufficiently clear and precise to programme into the expert system.

Carlson insists upon criteria which are even more difficult to meet. He uses experiential expertise rather than rules as the basis for his approach to expert systems in social work. He links competent problem solving to cognitive activity rather than to try to codify a full knowledge base: "social work should obtain greater benefit from trying to capture experience-based schema rather than trying to reduce such schema to rules. If the schema were developed by insightful clinicians, necessity should result in incorporation of an interactive focus" (Carlson, 1989: 46). Here he is aiming very high indeed. His approach, although theoretically impeccable, would be extremely burdensome to the human expert, and may well turn out to be impracticable.

Schuerman and Vogel introduce a note of caution into the debate on expert systems. They remind us that the process of transferring human expertise to computers (a process they call "knowledge engineering") can be problematic:

> Knowledge engineering in the human services may be difficult, given the lack of congruence among experts about the problems presented by particular cases. A group of professional child welfare workers may agree on who is or is not an expert in their setting but the experts themselves may not agree on important aspects of placement planning. For example, experts may disagree about what facts to elicit in conducting an assessment of a child and family. Even with agreement about which facts to use, experts may differ in the interpretation they attach to specific facts. Further, even with agreement about the selection and interpretation of facts, experts may disagree about the placement recommendations that follow from given facts (Schuerman and Vogel, 1986: 539).

The important issue, though, is that knowledge engineering is in its infancy and that all but the most straightforward social work tasks are a tough nut to crack.

Example: A Welfare Benefits Expert System

Welfare Benefit programmes using expert systems techniques have considerable advantages over more conventional ones. For example, the fact that the programme's knowledge of benefit regulations is specified entirely in the rules themselves and that these rules are intelligible to people who are not experts in computer programming means that it is relatively easy to maintain the programme in the face of frequent minor changes to the regulations. It is also possible to show a simplified form of the rules to the user and, in particular, to display the specific rules which led to a conclusion, thus helping to convey the reasons behind the machine's recommendations. In principle, the system could also tell users what the implications of their answers are, so that they could see the purpose of the system's questions and respond with that in mind, although there are as yet few examples of systems as sophisticated as this (Dawson, Buckland and Gilbert, 1987).

Let us look how such an expert system would look like from the point of view of the client. The Alvey DHSS Demonstrator project was established in late 1984 to show how advanced IT could be applied in large organisations like the United Kingdom Department of Health and Social Security (DHSS). It was an expert system on the public provision of welfare benefit advice. Two questions were asked:

1) Do public attitudes reflect a version of technological determinism that computers are undesirable no matter what their purpose?
2) If the public will accept computers in general, would actual and potential social security claimants use computers to get welfare benefit advice?

In answering the first question which is of only general interest to us Dawson et al. (1987) found that there was general agreement that computer technology would play an increasingly important role in people's lives and that there was a tendency to balance the advantages and disadvantages of computer technology.

Of greater interest is the conditions of acceptance of a welfare benefit advice system. They found that the four main advantages of a welfare benefit advice system identified by the public were:

1) a more impersonal service in answering sensitive questions on income and house composition;
2) access to advice locally with easy access and privacy;
3) accurate and comprehensive benefit information;
4) procedural advice so as to be better informed when dealing with DHSS personnel.

The first two advantages refer to the characteristics of the use of the technology. What the potential clients are describing here is the advantage to them of machine over humans from their personal perspective of a user. The potential for a computer to depersonalise the process of claiming benefits was viewed as a wholly positive outcome. This is an interesting point because "depersonalising" is generally viewed as being negative. Thus the social context within which the computer is used provides the perspective whether its depersonalising tendency is a positive or negative phenomenon. Potential clients of the welfare benefit advice system also stated that the computer should afford privacy – another indicator of the importance of depersonalisation in the welfare benefit advice process.

The last two advantages refer to the content of the information which the computer can provide and it is here that the potential clients are describing the characteristics of a useful expert system.

Two main forms of help were identified which the system should provide: information on benefit entitlement; and procedural information on where to go and how to apply for particular benefits. Ideally this information would need to be

1) comprehensive, covering not just one but the whole range of state benefits currently available to members of the public;
2) accurate and up-to-date, so that users are not given misinformation on which to base their decisions on whether to claim;
3) intelligible, in being easily understood rather than in administrative jargon;
4) confidential, in that all information fed into and extracted from the system should be confidential to the user.

They found that procedural information also must be part of the expert system: "Claimants need to know about the mechanics of claiming, such as whether an application can be made by post, whether an interview is required, whether or not it is possible to arrange a home visit, the identification number of the application form and the nature and type of information that would have to be disclosed" (Dawson et al., 1987: 16).

This type of expert system redefines the power relationship between welfare officials and claimants. An expert system is a method of empowerment transferring knowledge from a selected few to the many. Dawson et al. conclude their discussion with the following upbeat assessment: "by distributing knowledge to the public, rather than containing knowledge within the boundaries of the organisation, there is a possibility that, if claimants become more confident about their rightful entitlement, the experience of claiming may become less humiliating" (Dawson et al., 1987: 18).

Example: BRIEFER: An Expert System for Clinical Practice

BRIEFER (Goodman, Gingerich and de Shazer, 1989) is a prototype expert system which is designed to advise family therapists at the Brief Family Therapy Center (Milwaukee, Wisconsin, USA) on which intervention to give clients at the conclusion of the first therapy session. Brief therapy is a short-term (4-6 sessions) systematic approach to therapy which focuses on solutions rather than problems. The therapist attempts to help the client to identify what a suitable solution would be. Brief therapy takes place with a client, a therapy team and an interview room with an adjoining consulting room separated by a one-way mirror. The overall strategy, and the specific interventions which implement the therapy, are based on two sources of information: the information elicited during the interview and the specialised knowledge of the therapy team.

The problem selected for the expert system was one to aid the therapist in deciding on the intervention to be made at the end of the first session. The expert system was to function as the team does during the consulting break when the primary therapist confers with the team about what intervention to give the client. The problem selected for the expert system was a suitable one as it would enable the primary therapist to work without the expert team thereby making scarce expertise more widely available.

The next step in the development of the expert system was to extract the knowledge of the human experts so that it can be programmed into the computer. The knowledge that went into the expert system was developed from several sources: the knowledge and experience of the human experts, the professional literature, and the analysis of actual cases. As we saw above, it was found that although experts possess the expertise needed to solve a given problem, often they cannot describe the procedures they follow clearly and precisely to programme an expert system.

Knowledge is represented in the expert system according to a rule-based scheme. Goodman et al. (1989) report that in a rule-based system, knowledge is represented in a series in *if-then* rules. This means that *if* the conditions are true, *then* the conclusion is also true. BRIEFER uses a system where all the facts *(ifs)* for a case are collected and on the bases of the facts the conclusions *(thens)* are deduced. Once BRIEFER has asked its questions it compares the responses to the conditions of each of the rules in an attempt to reach conclusions. BRIEFER then gives its recommendation. BRIEFER can then ask if the user (therapist) would like an explanation of any of the recommendations given. BRIEFER can do this by printing out the text which is the IFs and THENs of the rule.

The evaluation of BRIEFER was quite positive. Goodman (1986) reported that an evaluation of 12 cases found that the advice given by BRIEFER closely paralleled the intervention given by the human experts except for some cases involving complex problems. While BRIEFER rarely offers advice which the experienced therapist had not already thought of it does appear helpful to trainees or inexperienced therapists.

Conclusions

After spending much of the book cataloguing problems and difficulties in the introduction of IT to the social services it is good to be able to end on a high note with positive examples of successful practice. Decision support systems have already started to make their mark and their is light at the end of the tunnel with regard to expert systems. They do have a useful role to play in the rule-bound and technical (but by no means clear-cut) world of welfare benefits. And there are some positive signs in at least one area in social work practice *per se.*

Epilogue

Information Technology in the Service of the Social Services: a Value Orientation

The unique professional identity and moral worth of social work depends upon the integrity of its value base. Social work values need to be maintained and nurtured during major organisational transformations. As we have seen in this book, the introduction of IT into social work is a a major change indeed. In this context the goal is to establish a social setting where harmonisation between IT and social work values can be maximised.

At first sight, harmonisation may appear difficult to achieve. In a humanistic profession the role of technology as a form of human knowledge created for doing things and solving problems can be seen as intimidating. But responding to social change within a secure value framework is not threatening. It is the internalisation of the unique identity and values of social work which enables it to apply IT in a human way.

Harmonising IT with social work values raises issues regarding the delicate balance between those aspects of social work which are within the autonomy of the profession itself and those which relate to the roles it has to fulfil in order to discharge its agency functions. Most IT implementations are initiated by managers for the purpose of enhancing agency efficiency. There is a danger that the results of this process will affect the ethos of social work itself and the professional identity of social workers.

The achievement of harmonisation depends on consensus building which is in itself an operationalisation of an element of social work's value base. This includes empowerment, devolution in decision-making and establishing free access to knowledge. The results of the process should be the operational definition of harmonisation: the use of IT in a social service setting in accordance with social work values.

We believe that the following elements are central to harmonious implementation of IT in social work

1) A *humanistic organisational setting*. This implies that IT has to fit into a people-oriented, flexible, and at times informal setting.

2) *Consensus building*. This is essential in defining the goals and role of IT in social work.

3) *Maximum decentralising of decision-making*. This increases participation at all levels.

4) *Empowerment of social workers and clients*. While the organisation may function formally in a top-down manner, empowerment of the different levels of the social service organisation indicates the dominance of humanistic values.

5) *Equality in access of knowledge as a resource*. The right to know and to be an equal partner in the decision-making process humanises the social service setting. Working with and not working for is a theme.

6) *Continued involvement of management, social workers, and service users in the IT change process*. The dynamics of organisational change are such that the results of a once-off involvement exercise will soon become dissipated and useless.

The result of this harmonisation perspective is that IT is not perceived as a threat to the inherent nature of social work. Social workers use IT within their value framework without the fear of their tasks becoming technological or administrative in nature. The result is that IT does not dominate social work but rather becomes an instrument for helping social work be more effective. IT becomes an enabler for the implementation of services which could not have been provided without it.

Bibliography

Anderson, James E. (1975) *Public Policy-Making*. New York: Praeger Publishers.

Barnard, Chester A. (1938) *The Functions of the Executive*. Cambridge, Mass.: Harvard University Press.

Benbenishty, Rami (1989) 'Designing Computerized Clinical Information Systems to Monitor Interventions on the Agency Level', pp. 69-88 in Cnaan, Ram A./Parsloe, Phyllida (eds.) *The Impact of Information Technology on Social Work Practice*. New York: Haworth Press.

Benbenishty, Rami/Ben-Zaken, Anat (1988) 'Computer-Aided Process of Monitoring Task-Centred Family Interventions', *Social Work Research and Abstracts* 24/1: 7-9.

Ben-Tuvia, S./Deychev, E./Dor, I. (1988) *Classification of Local Authorities According to the Socio-Economic Characteristics of the Population*. Jerusalem: Central Bureau of Statistics.

Berman, Yitzhak (1991) 'BARAK: An Information Technology Program for the Local Social Service Department', in Berman, Yitzhak (ed.) *Information Technology in Local Social Service Departments in Israel*. Jerusalem: ENITH-Israel.

Berman, Yitzhak (1992) 'A Decision Support System in Resource Allocation: The Political Process in Rational Decision Making', *New Technology in the Human Services* 6/1: 8-14.

Berman, Y./Eaglstein, A.S. (1993) 'IT Use by a Central Welfare Administration: The Israeli Experience', HUSITA-3 Conference: *Information Technology and the Quality of Life and Services*, Maastricht, The Netherlands, 15-18 June 1993.

Berman, Y./Phillips, D. (1993) 'Two Faces of Information Technology: What Does the Social Worker See in the Mirror?', HUSITA-3 Conference: *Information Technology and the Quality of Life and Services*, Maastricht, The Netherlands, 15-18 June 1993.

Berman, Y./Phillips, D. (1994) 'Implementing a Computerised Social Services Information System', *Research, Policy and Planning* 12/1: 10-15.

Bevan, Edis, (1988) 'The Task for a New Professionalism', pp. 332-341 in Glastonbury, Bryan/LaMendola, Walter/Toole, Stuart (eds.) *Information Technology and the Human Services*. Chichester: Wiley.

Blau, Peter M. (1955) *The Dynamics of Bureaucracy*. Chicago: University of Chicago Press.

Blazyk, Stan/Wimberley, Edward T./Crawford, Carla (1987) 'Computer-Based Case Management for the Elderly', *Computers in Human Services* 2/1-2: 63-77.

Booth, Tim (1986) 'Social Research and Policy Relevance', *Research Policy and Planning* 4/1-2: 15-18.

Booth, Tim (1988) *Developing Social Policy Research*. Aldershot: Gower.

Boyd Jr., Lawrence H./Hylton, John H./Price, Steven V. (1978) 'Computers in Social Work Practice: A Review', *Social Work* 23/5: 368-371.

Brauns, Hans-Jochen/Kramer, David (1981) 'Social Work in an Information Society: New Challenges and Opportunities', pp. 143-151 in Nowotny, H. (ed.) *The Information Society: Its Impact on the Home, Local Community and Marginal Groups*. Vienna: European Centre for Social Welfare Training and Research.

Brauns, Hans-Jochen/Kramer, David (1987) 'Information Technology and Social Work Education in the 1980s: Three Theses', *International Social Work* 30: 129-138.

Brightman, Harvey J./Harris, Sidney E. (1985) 'Is your Information System Mature Enough for Computerized Planning', *Long Range Planning* 18/5: 68-73.

Brinckmann, Hans (1988) 'Rise or Fall of the Expert: The Position of the Service Worker in an High Tech Environment', *New Technology in the Human Services* 4/2: 19-24.

Bronson, Denise E./Pelz, Donald C./Trzcinski, Eileen (1988) *Computerizing Your Agency's Information System*. Sage Human Services Guide, 54. Newbury Park: Sage.

Burns, Tom/Stalker, G. M. (1961) *The Management of Innovation*. London: Tavistock.

Burrell, Gibson/Morgan, Gareth (1979) *Sociological Paradigms and Organisational Analysis*. London: Heinemann.

Butterfield, William H. (1986) 'Computers in Social Work and Social Welfare: Issues and Perspectives', *Journal of Sociology and Social Welfare* 13/1: 5-26.

Calista, Donald J. (1986) 'Linking Policy Intention and Policy Implementation: The Role of the Organization in the Integration of Human Services', *Administration and Society* 18/2: 263-286.

Caputo, Richard K. (1988) *Management and Information Systems in Human Services: Implications for the Distribution of Authority and Decision Making*. New York: Haworth Press.

Caputo, Richard K. (1991) 'Managing Information Systems: An Ethical Framework and Information Needs Matrix', *Administration in Social Work* 15/4: 53-64.

Carlson, Raymond W. (1989) 'Capturing Expertise in Clinical Information Processing', pp. 37-52 in Cnaan, Ram A./Parsloe, Phyllida (eds.) *The Impact of Information Technology on Social Work Practice*. New York: Haworth Press.

Carragone, P./Austin, D. (1981) *Final Report: A Comparative Study of the Functions of the Case Manager in Multi-Purpose, Comprehensive and Categorical Programs*. Austin, School of Social Work, University of Texas at Austin.

Carrilio, Terry E./Kasser, Judith/Moretto, Anthony H. (1985) 'Management Information Systems: Who is in Charge?', *Social Casework: Journal of Contemporary Social Work* 66/7: 417-423.

Challis, Linda (1988) *Joint Approaches to Social Policy*. Cambridge: Cambridge University Press.

Chambers, R. (1982) *Rural Development: Putting the Last First*. London: Longman.

Chelimsky, E. (1983) 'The Definition and Measurement of Evaluation Quality as a Management Tool', in St. Pierre, R.G. (ed.) *Management and Organisation of Program Evaluation*. San Francisco: Jossey Bass.

Chinoy, Ely (1967) *Society*. New York: Random House.

Christensen, Kathleen E. (1986) 'Ethics of Information Technology', pp. 72-91 in Geiss, Gunther R./Viswanathan, Narayan (eds.) (1986) *The Human Edge: Information Technology and Helping People*. New York: Haworth Press.

Chubon, Robert A. (1986) 'Genesis II: A Computer-Based Case Management Simulation', *Rehabilitation Counseling Bulletin* 30/1: 25-32.

Clark, Carlton, F. (1988) 'Computer Applications in Social Work', *Social Work Research and Abstracts* 24/1: 15-19.

Clark, Sheila, (1987) 'A Micro-Menu for Macro Planning', *Computer Applications in Social Work* 3/4: 3-6.

Cnaan, Ram A. (1988a) 'Computer Illiteracy and Human Services', *New Technology in the Human Services* 4/1: 3-8.

Cnaan, Ram A. (1988b) 'Application of Computers in Clinical Supervision', pp. 128-136 in Glastonbury, Bryan/LaMendola, Walter/Toole, Stuart (eds.) *Information Technology and the Human Services*. Chichester: Wiley.

Cnaan, Ram A. (1989a) 'Introduction: Social Work Practice and Information Technology – An Unestablished Link', pp. 1-16 in Cnaan, Ram A./Parsloe, Phyllida (eds.) *The Impact of Information Technology on Social Work Practice*. New York: Haworth Press.

Cnaan, Ram A. (1989b) 'Social Work Education and Direct Practice in the Computer Age', *Journal of Social Work Education* 25/3: 235-243.

Cnaan, Ram A./Parsloe, Phyllida (eds.) (1989) *The Impact of Information Technology on Social Work Practice*. New York: Haworth Press.

Collins, B. (1986) 'Defining Feminist Social Work Practice', *Social Work* 31: 214-221.

Colombi, D. P. (1993) *Computer Applications for the Probation Service*. Southampton, PhD. thesis, University of Southampton.

Cordingley, Elizabeth (1986) 'Patterns of Computer use in the UK', pp. 25-45 in Horobin, G./Montgomery, S. (eds) *New Information Technology in Management and Practice*. Research Highlights in Social Work 13. London: Kogan Page.

Cotter, B. (1981) *Planning and Implementing Social Service Information Systems: A Guide for Management and Users*. Project Share, Department of Health and Human Services, DHHS Monograph Series 25, DHEW Publication NO. OS-76-130. Washington D.C.: Government Printing Office.

Cwikel, Julie G./Cnaan, Ram A. (1991) 'Ethical Dilemmas in Applying Second-Wave Information Technology to Social Work Practice', *Social Work* 36/2: 114-120.

Dawson, Patrick/Buckland, Sarah/Gilbert, Nigel (1987) 'Expert Systems and the Public Provision of Welfare Benefit Advice', Paper presented to the British Sociological Association Annual Conference at the University of Leeds.

Dean, Ruth G./Fenby, Barbara L. (1989) 'Exploring Epistemologies: Social Work Action as a Reflection of Philosophical Assumptions', *Journal of Social Work Education* 25/1: 46-54.

de Graaf, Hein (1987) 'Computers in the Dutch Social Services', *Computer Applications in Social Work and Allied Professions* 3/4: 15-19.

de Silva, Richard (1992) 'Bits, Bytes and Foul-ups', *Newsweek,* 21 September.

Dove, Roger (1989) 'Implementing a New System: The Importance of Training', *New Technology in the Human Services* 4/3: 12-15.

du Feu, David (1982) *Computers and Social Workers: The Reception of a Computerised Client Record System in Social Services Fieldwork District Offices*. Edinburgh, PhD. thesis, University of Edinburgh.

Eaden, Martin (1990) 'Information Needs of Case Managers, The Information Challenge for Community Care', *Association of Directors of Social Work/ICL,* Seminar, Queen Margaret College, Edinburgh, pp. 20-22.

Eaglstein A.S./Berman, Y. (1993) 'Information Technology Use by a Central Welfare Administration: The Israeli Experience', HUSITA-3 Conference: *IT and the Quality of Life and Services,* Maastricht, The Netherlands, June 15-17 1993.

Eaglstein, A. S./Pardes, Y. (1983) 'A Formula for Determining Social Worker Positions Based on the Pardes Method', *Social Indicators Research* 13: 59-68.

Eastman, Beva (1991) 'Women, Computers, and Social Change', *Computers in Human Services* 8/1: 41-53.

ENITH (European Network for Information Technology and Human Services) (1992) *European Resource Book.* Utrecht: NIZW.

Epstein, Joyce (1984) *New Technology – New Entitlement: an Experiment in Public Access Computers to Assess Entitlement to Benefit.* London: Research Institute for Consumer Affairs.

Epstein, Joyce, (1988) 'Information Systems and the Consumer', pp. 13-26 in Glastonbury, Bryan/LaMendola, Walter/Toole, Stuart (eds.) *Information Technology and the Human Services.* Chichester: Wiley.

Epstein, William M. (1986) 'Science and Social Work', *Social Service Review* 60/1: 145-160.

Erdman, Harold P./Klein, Marjorie H./Griest, John H. (1985) 'Direct Patient Computer Interviewing', *Journal of Counselling and Clinical Psychology* 33/6: 760-775.

Finn, J. (1988) 'Microcomputers in Private, Nonprofit Agencies', *Social Work Research and Abstracts* 24/1: 10-14.

Finnegan, Daniel J./Ivanoff, Andre (1991) 'Effects of Brief Computer Training on Attitudes Toward Computer Use in Practice: An Educational Experiment', *Journal of Social Work Education* 27/1: 73-82.

Finnegan, Daniel J./Ivanoff, Andre/Smyth, Nancy J. (1991) 'The Computer Applications Explosion: What Practitioners and Clinical Managers Need to Know', *Computers in Human Services* 8/2: 1-19.

Flynn, M. L. (1977) 'Computer-based Instruction in Social Policy: A One-Year Trial', *Journal of Education for Social Work* 13: 52-59.

Flynn, Norman/Miller, Clive (1991) *Caring in our Communities: The Management Agenda.* London: National Institute for Social Work Information Service.

Forrest, Jan/Williams, Sandra (1987) *New Technology and Information Exchange in Social Services.* London: Policy Studies Institute.

Fraser, Mark/Taylor, Mary Jane/Jackson, Robert/O'Jack, Jamal (1991) 'Social Work and Science: Many Ways of Knowing?', *Social Work Research and Abstracts* 27/45: 15.

Frans, D. J. (1989) *The Diffusion on Information Technology and Social Work Empowerment.* Denver, Ph.D. Dissertation, University of Denver.

Freedberg, Sharon (1989) 'Self-Determination: Historical Perspectives and Effects on Current Practice', *Social Work* 34/1: 33-38.

Gandy, John M./Tepperman, Lorne (1990) *False Alarm: The Computerization of Eight Social Welfare Organizations.* Waterloo (Ontario): Wilfred Laurier University Press.

Garrett, William J. (1986) 'Information Technology in Direct Service to Clients', pp. 235-253 in Geiss, Gunther R./Viswanathan, Narayan (eds.) *The Human Edge: Information Technology and Helping People.* New York: Haworth Press.

Geiss, Gunther (1983) 'Some Thoughts about the Future: Information Technology and Social Work Practice', *Practice Digest* 6: 33-35.

Geiss, Gunther R./Viswanathan, Narayan (eds.) (1986) *The Human Edge: Information Technology and Helping People.* New York: Haworth Press.

Gingerich, Wallace, J. (1990a) 'Expert Systems: New Tools for Decision-Making', *Computers in Human Services* 6/4: 219-230.

Gingerich, Wallace, J. (1990b) 'Developing Expert Systems', *Computers in Human Services* 6/4: 251-264.

Gingerich, Wallace/Schirtzinger, Janet/Hoffman, David L. (1991) 'MY ASSISTANT: Design and Development of A Computer-Assisted Case Management System', paper presented at the *Second Human Service Information Technology Applications* (HUSITA-2) International Conference, New Brunswick, New Jersey, June 26-30, 1991.

Glaser, E. M./Abelson, H. H./Garrison, K. N. (1983) *Putting Knowledge to Use: Facilitating the Diffusion of Knowledge and the Implementation of Planned Change.* San Francisco: Jossey-Bass.

Glastonbury, Bryan (1985) *Computers in Social Work.* London: Macmillan.

Glastonbury, Bryan (1986) 'Managing the Social Services Computer System: Some Problems and Pitfalls', *Computer Applications in Social Work and Allied Professions* 3/1: 10-13.

Glastonbury, Bryan, (1988) 'Policy Development and Administration', pp. 184-190 in Glastonbury, Bryan/LaMendola, Walter/Toole, Stuart (eds.) *Information Technology and the Human Services.* Chichester: Wiley.

Glastonbury, Bryan (1990) 'Up Front', *New Technology in the Human Services* 5/2: 1-3.

Glastonbury, Bryan/LaMendola, Walter/Toole, Stuart (eds.) (1988) *Information Technology and the Human Services.* Chichester: Wiley.

Glennerster, Howard/Power, Anne/Travers, Tony (1991) 'A New Era for Social Policy: A New Enlightenment or a New Leviathan?', *Journal of Social Policy* 20/3: 389-414.

Goldstein, Howard (1986) 'Toward the Integration of Theory and Practice: A Humanistic Approach', *Social Work* 31/5: 352-357.

Goldstein, Howard (1990) 'The Knowledge Base of Social Work Practice: Theory, Wisdom, Analogue or Art?', *Families in Society: The Journal of Contemporary Human Services* 71/1: 32-43.

Goodman, H. (1986) *BRIEFER: An Expert System for Brief Family Therapy.* Milwaukee, Master's thesis, University of Wisconsin-Milwaukee.

Goodman, Hannah/Gingerich, Wallace J./de Shazer, Steve (1989) 'BRIEFER: An Expert System for Clinical Practice', pp. 53-68 in Cnaan, Ram A./Parsloe, Phyllida (eds.) *The Impact of Information Technology on Social Work Practice.* New York: Haworth Press.

Gorry, A. G./Morton, M. S. (1971) 'A Framework for Management Information Systems', *Sloan Management Review* 13: 55-70.

Gripton, James (1983) 'Computerizing Your Practice', *Practice Digest* 6: 16-20.

Gripton, James/Licker, Paul (1986) 'Apply Computers to Clinical Social Work', *Journal of Sociology and Social Welfare* 13/1: 27-55.

Gripton, James/Licker, Paul/de Groot, Leo (1988) 'Microcomputers in Clinical Social Work', pp. 76-96 in Glastonbury, Bryan/LaMendola, Walter/Toole, Stuart (eds.) *Information Technology and the Human Services.* Chichester: Wiley.

Grisham, M./White, M./Miller, L. S. (1983) 'Case Management as a Problem-Solving Strategy', *Pride Institute Journal of Long-Term Health Care* 2/4: 21-28.

Grosser, Charles F. (1973) *New Directions in Community Organization: From Enabling to Advocacy*. New York, Praeger Publishers.

Gunn, Mike (1989) 'Information Systems Design', *New Technology in the Human Services* 4/3: 15-18.

Habib, J. (undated) *The Supply and Demand for Social Work Manpower, Memorandum for the Committee on the Status of the Social Worker*. Waltham, Mass.: Brandies University.

Hammer, Allen L./Hile, Metthew G. (1985) 'Factors in Clinicians Resistance to Automation in Mental Health', *Computers in Human Services* 1/3: 1-25.

Hasenfeld, Yeheskel (1983) *Human Services Organizations*. Englewood Cliffs, New Jersey: Prentice Hall.

Hasenfeld, Yeheskel (1987) 'Power in Social Work Practice', *Social Service Review* 61/ 3: 469-483.

Hegar, Rebecca L. (1989) 'Empowerment-Based Practice with Children', *Social Service Review* 63/3: 372-383.

Hegar, Rebecca L./Hunzeker, Jeanne M. (1988) 'Moving Toward Empowerment-Based Practice in Public Child Welfare', *Social Work* 33/6: 499-502.

Hernandez, Santos H./Leung, Patrick (1990) 'Implementing a Social Work Curriculum on Information Technology', *Computers in Human Services* 7/1-2: 113-125.

Highfill, John/Mundle, George/Page, Charles/Armentrout, Edmund (1986) 'Multi-Agency Information Management for Human Services', *American Planners Association Journal* Winter: 76-82.

Hirayama, Hisashi/Centingok, Muammer (1988) 'Empowerment: A Social Work Approach for Asian Immigrants', *Social Casework* 69/1: 41-47.

HMSO (1989) *Caring for People: Community Care in the Next Decade and Beyond*. London: Her Majesty's Stationary Office.

HMSO (1990) *National Health Service and Community Care Act 1990*. London: Her Majesty's Stationary Office.

Hogwood, Brian W./Peters, B. Guy (1982) 'The Dynamics of Policy Change: Policy Succession', *Policy Sciences* 14/1: 225-245.

Holbrook, Terry, (1986) 'Computer Technology – 1984 and Beyond', *Journal of Sociology and Social Welfare* 13/1: 98-114.

Holbrook, Terry, (1988) 'Computer Technology and Behavior Therapy: a Modern Marriage', *Computers in Human Services* 3/1-2: 89-109.

Holbrook, Terry (1990) 'Managing Consent in the Computer Age', pp. 107-119 in Pardeck, John T./Murphy, John W. (eds.) *Computers in Human Services: An Overview for Clinical and Welfare Services*. Chur: Harwood Academic Publishers.

Homer, Garry/Schoech, Dick (1988) 'System Design and Development', pp. 279-283 in Glastonbury, Bryan/LaMendola, Walter/Toole, Stuart (eds.) *Information Technology and the Human Services*. Chichester: Wiley.

Hooyman, Nancy R./Nurius, Paula S./Nicoll, Anne E. (1990) 'The Perspective from the Field on Computer Literacy Training Needs', *Computers in Human Services* 7/1-2: 95-112.

Howe, David (1987) *An Introduction to Social Work Theory*. Aldershot: Wildwood House.

Imre, R. W. (1982) *Knowing and Caring: Philosophical Issues in Social Work*. Lanham MD: University Press of America.

Imre, Roberta Wells (1984) 'The Nature of Knowledge in Social Work', *Social Work* 29/
    1: 41-45.
Isaksson, Tommy (1991) *The BITS-Project: Child Care in the Admass Society*. Sweden:
    University College of Falun/Borlange.
Janson, Fred V./Lewis, Robert E. (1990) 'Spreadsheet Analysis in Human Services',
    Computers in Human Services 6/1-3: 51-68.
Karger, H. Jacob (1983) 'Science, Research and Social Work: Who Controls the
    Profession?', *Social Work* 28/3: 200-205.
Karger, Howard Jacob/Kreuger, Larry W. (1988) 'Technology and the "Not Always So
    Human" Services', *Computers in Human Services* 3/1-2: 111-126.
Keen, P. G. W./Scott Morton, M. S. (1978) *Decision Support Systems: An Organizational
    Perspective*. Reading MA: Addison-Wesley.
Kling, Rob (1980) 'Social Analysis of Computing: Theoretical Perspectives in Recent
    Empirical Research', *Computing Surveys* 12: 61-110.
Kopp, Judy (1989) 'Self-Observation: An Empowerment Strategy in Assessment', *Social
    Casework* 70/5: 276-284.
Koroloff, Nancy M. (1989) 'Implementing an Information System in a Human Service
    Organization: Integrating People, Procedures and Equipment', pp. 287-297 in
    LaMendola, Walter/Glastonbury, Bryan/Toole, Stuart (eds.) *A Casebook of Computer
    Applications in the Social and Human Services*. New York: Haworth Press.
Kraut, Robert/Dumais, Susan/Koch, Susan (1989) 'Computerization, Productivity and
    Quality of Work Life', *Communications of the ACM* 32: 220.
Kraemer, Kenneth L./Danziger, James N. (1984) 'Computers and Control in the Work
    Environment', *Public Administration Review* 44/1: 32-42.
Kreuger, Larry/Stretch, John J. (1990) 'Human Services and Computers: Management and
    Staff Adjustments', pp. 97-105 in Pardeck, John T./Murphy, John W. (eds.) *Computers
    in Human Services: An Overview for Clinical and Welfare Services*. Chur: Harwood
    Academic Publishers.
Kucic, A. Ronald/Sorensen, James E./Hanbery, Glyn W. (1983) 'Computer Selection for
    Human Service Organizations', *Administration in Social Work* 7/1: 63-75.
Lamb, Jane Adams (1990) 'Teaching Computer Literacy to Human Services Students',
    Computers in Human Services 7/1-2: 31-45.
LaMendola, Walter, (1986) 'Software Development in the USA', *Computer Applications
    in Social Work* 3/1, 2-7.
LaMendola, Walter (1987) 'Teaching Information Technology to Social Workers', *Journal
    of Teaching in Social Work* 1/1: 53-69.
LaMendola, Walter/Glastonbury, Bryan/Toole, Stuart (1989) 'Service Provision and
    Delivery and Information Technology', pp. 9-27 in LaMendola, Walter/Glastonbury,
    Bryan/Toole, Stuart (eds.) *A Casebook of Computer Applications in the Social and
    Human Services*. New York: Haworth Press.
Layton, Edwin T. Jr. (1974) 'Technology as Knowledge', *Technology and Culture* 15/1:
    31-41.
Layton, Edwin T. Jr. (1987) 'Through the Looking glass, or News from Lake Mirror Image',
    Technology and Culture 28: 594-607.
Leiderman, Marcos/Guzetta, Charles/Struminger, Leny/Monnickendam, Menachem (eds.)
    (1993) *Technology in People Services: Research, Theory and Applications*. New York:
    Haworth Press.

Levitan, Karen, B./Willis, Elizabeth A. (1985) 'Barriers to Practitioners' Use of Information Technology Utilization: A Discussion of the Results of a Study', pp. 21-34 in Figley, Charles R. (ed.) *Computers and Family Therapy*. New York: Haworth Press.

Lindsey, Duncan/Kirk, Stuart A. (1992) 'The Role of Social Work Journals in the Development of a Knowledge Base for the Profession', *Social Service Review* 66/2: 295-310.

Lingham, Richard/Law, Mark (1989) 'Using Computers for Better Administration of Social Services Departments', pp. 117-132 in Cnaan, Ram A./Parsloe, Phyllida (eds.) *The Impact of Information Technology on Social Work Practice*. New York, Haworth Press.

Lohmann, Roger A./Wolvovsky, Jay (1979) 'Natural Language Processing and Computer Use in Social Work', *Administration in Social Work* 3/4: 409-423.

MacBride, S. (ed.) (1980) *Many Voices, One World: Towards a New, More Just and More Efficient World Communication Order*. Paris: UNESCO and Kogan Page.

MacFadden, Robert James (1986) 'The Microcomputer Millennium: Transforming the Small Social Agency', *Social Casework* 67/3: 160-165.

McNown, Robert (1986) 'On the Uses of Econometric Models: A Guide for Policy Makers', *Policy Sciences* 19: 359-380.

Macarov, D. (1990) 'Confidentiality in the Human Services', *International Journal of Sociology and Social Policy* 10/4-6: 65-81.

Mandell, Steven F. (1989) 'Resistance and Power: The Perceived Effect that Computerization has on a Social Agency's Power Relationship', *Computers in Human Services* 4/1-2: 29-40.

Markus, Elliot J. (1990) 'Computerisation: A Precondition for, or a Product of, Responsible Social Work Practice', *International Journal of Sociology and Social Policy* 10/4-6: 30-53.

Marlett, Nancy (1988) 'Empowerment Through Computer Telecommunications', pp. 244-264 in Glastonbury, Bryan/LaMendola, Walter/Toole, Stuart (eds.) *Information Technology and the Human Services*. Chichester: Wiley.

Marsh, Peter/Omerod, Bill/Roberts, Jane (1986) 'Introducing Information Technology in Social Service Departments', *Computer Applications in Social Work and Allied Professions* 3/2: 1-5.

Matheson, A.D. (1991) 'Innovative Use of Computers for Planning in Human Service Organizations', paper prepared for the *Second Human Service Information Technology Applications* (HUSITA-2) International Conference, New Brunswick, New Jersey, June 26-30, 1991.

Matheson, A.D. (1993) 'Innovative Use of Computers for Planning in Human Service Organizations', pp. 383-395 in Leiderman, Marcos/Guzetta, Charles/Struminger, Leny/Monnickendam, Menachem (eds.) *Technology in People Services: Research, Theory and Applications*. New York: Haworth Press.

Mathisen, Werner Christie (1990) 'The Problem-Solving Community', *Knowledge: Creation, Diffusion, Utilization* 11/4: 410-427.

Meyer, Marshall W. (1968) 'Automation and Bureaucratic Structure', *American Journal of Sociology* 74: 254-264.

Minahan, A. (1976) 'Generalists and Specialists in Social Work – Implications for Education and Practice', *Arete* 4/2: 62.

Monnickendam, Menachem (1989) 'Developing an Integrated Computerized Case Management System for the Israeli Defence Forces – an Evolutionary Approach', pp. 133-149 in Cnaan, Ram A./Parsloe, Phyllida (eds.) *The Impact of Information Technology on Social Work Practice*. New York: Haworth Press.

Monnickendam, Menachem/Berman, Yitzhak (1985) 'Information Systems in the Personal Social Services in Israel', *Computer Applications in Social Work* 2/3: 41-52.

Monnickendam, Menachem/Cnaan, Ram A. (1990) 'Teaching Information Technology to Human Service Students: Meeting the Needs of the Future', *Computers in Human Services* 7/1-2: 149-163.

Monnickendam, Menachem/Eaglstein, A. Solomon (1992) 'Computer Acceptance by Social Workers: Some Unexpected Research Findings', Paper presented at the *Second Human Service Information Technology Applications* (HUSITA-2) International Conference, New Brunswick, New Jersey, June 26-30, 1991.

Monnickendam, Menachem/Eaglstein, A. Solomon (1993) 'Computer Acceptance by Social Workers: Some Unexpected Research Findings', pp. 409-425 in Leiderman, Marcos/Guzetta, Charles/Struminger, Leny/Monnickendam, Menachem (eds.) *Technology in People Services: Research, Theory and Applications*. New York: Haworth Press.

Monnickendam, Menachem/Yaniv, H. (1989) 'The Knowledge Workstation for Human Service Practitioners', paper given to the International Experts' consultation on the *Use of Computers in Social Work*, November 5-9, 1989, Jerusalem, Israel.

Montgomery, Stuart, (1986) 'Implementing and Managing Computerised Client Information Systems', pp. 63-74 in Horobin, G./Montgomery, S. (eds.) *New Information Technology in Management and Practice*. Research Highlights in Social Work 13. London: Kogan Page.

Murphy, John W./Pardeck, John T. (1986) 'Technologically Mediated Therapy: A Critique', *Social Casework* 67: 605-612.

Murphy, John W./Pardeck, John T. (1988) 'The Computer Micro-World: Knowledge and Social Planning', *Computers in Human Services* 3/1-2: 127-141.

Murphy, John W./Pardeck, John T. (1989) 'Technology, Computerization, and the Conceptualization of Service Delivery', pp. 197-211 in Cnaan, Ram A./Parsloe, Phyllida (eds.) *The Impact of Information Technology on Social Work Practice*. New York: Haworth Press.

Murphy, John W./Pardeck, John T. (1990a) 'Introduction', pp. 1-8 in Murphy, John W./Pardeck, John T. (eds.) (1990) *Computers in Human Services: An Overview for Clinical and Welfare Services*. Chur: Harwood Academic Publishers.

Murphy, John W./Pardeck, John T. (1990b) 'An Analysis of Critical Concerns in the Use of Computer Technology in Clinical Practice', pp. 67-74 in Murphy, John W./Pardeck, John T. (eds.) *Computers in Human Services: An Overview for Clinical and Welfare Services*. Chur: Harwood Academic Publishers.

Murphy, John W./Pardeck, John T. (1990c) 'Expert Systems as an Adjunct to Clinical Practice: A Critique', pp. 75-86 in Murphy, John W./Pardeck, John T. (eds.) *Computers in Human Services: An Overview for Clinical and Welfare Services*. Chur: Harwood Academic Publishers.

Murphy, John W./Pardeck, John T. (1990d) 'Important Non-Technical Considerations in the Development of an MI System', pp. 129-136 in Murphy, John W./Pardeck, John T. (eds.) *Computers in Human Services: An Overview for Clinical and Welfare Services*. Chur: Harwood Academic Publishers.

Murphy, John W./Pardeck, John T./Nolan, Wesley L./Pilotta, Joseph J. (1987) 'Conceptual Issues Related to the Use of Computers in Social Work Practice', *Journal of Independent Social Work* 1/4: 67-73.

Mutschler, Elizabeth (1986) 'Patterns of Computer Use in the USA', pp. 46-62 in Horobin, G./Montgomery, S. (eds.) *New Information Technology in Management and Practice.* Research Highlights in Social Work 13. London: Kogan Page.

Mutschler, Elizabeth (1990) 'Computerized Information Systems for Social Workers in Health Care', *Health and Social Work* 15/3: 191-196.

Mutschler, Elizabeth/Cnaan, Ram A. (1985) 'Success and Failure of Computerized Information Systems: Two Case Studies in Human Service Agencies', *Administration in Social Work* 9/1: 67-79.

Mutschler, Elizabeth/Hansenfeld, Yechezkeil (1986) 'Integrated Information Systems for Social Work Practice', *Social Work* 31: 345-349.

Nakamura, Robert T. (1987) 'The Textbook Policy Process and Implementation Research', *Policy Studies Review* 7/1: 142-154.

National Association of Social Workers (1987a) *User's Guide to Social Work Abstracts.* Silver Spring, Maryland: National Association of Social Workers.

National Association of Social Workers (1987b) *Encyclopedia of Social Work*, 18th edition. Silver Spring, Maryland: National Association of Social Workers.

Newkham, J./Bawcom, L. (1981) 'Computerizing an Integrated Clinical and Financial Record System in a CMHC: A Pilot Project', *Administration in Social Work* 5/3-4: 97-112.

Nurius, Paula, S. (1990) 'Computer Literacy in Automated Assessment: Challenges and Future Directions', *Computers in Human Services* 6/4: 283-298.

Nurius, Paula/Cnaan, Ram A. (1991) 'Classifying Software to Better Support Social Work Practice', *Social Work* 36/6: 536-541.

Nurius, Paula/Hooyman, Nancy/Nicoll, Anne E. (1988) 'The Changing Face of Computer Utilization in Social Work Settings', *Journal of Social Work Education* 23/2: 186-197.

Nurius, Paula/Hooyman, Nancy/Nicoll, Anne E. (1991) 'Computers in Agencies: A Survey Baseline and Planning Implications', *Journal of Social Service Research* 14/3-4: 141-155.

Nurius, Paula/Hudson, Walter (1988) 'Computer Based Practice: Future Dream or Current Technology?', *Social Work* 33: 351-362.

Nurius, Paula/Hudson, Walter (1989) 'Computers and Social Diagnosis: the Client's Perspective', pp. 21-35 in Cnaan, Ram A./Parsloe, Phyllida (eds.) *The Impact of Information Technology on Social Work Practice.* New York: Haworth Press.

Nurius, Paula/Nicoll, Anne E. (1989) 'Computer Literacy Preparation: Conundrums and Opportunities for the Social Work Educator', *Journal of Teaching in Social Work* 3/2: 65-81.

Nurius, P. J./Richey, C. A./Nicoll, A. E., (1988) 'Preparation for Computer Usage in Social Work – Student Consumer Variables', *Journal of Social Work Education* 24/1: 60-69.

Oklahoma Department of Human Services (1989) *Families' Introduction to Integrated Services.* Oklahoma Department of Human Services. Oklahoma City.

Paley, John/Topping, Phil (1985) 'Computer Networks and Social Work Learning: A Perspective', pp. 16-24 in *Computer-Assisted Learning in Social Work Education and Training.* London: Central Council for Education and Training in Social Work.

Parayil, Govindan (1991) 'Technology as Knowledge: An Empirical Affirmation', *Knowledge: Creation, Diffusion, Utilization* 13./1: 36-48.

Pardeck, John, T. (1990) 'Computer Technology in Clinical Practice: An Overview of Ethical Concerns', pp. 55-65 in Pardeck, John T./Murphy, John W. (eds.) *Computers in Human Services: An Overview for Clinical and Welfare Services*. Chur: Harwood Academic Publishers.

Pardeck, John T./Stone Schulte, Ruth (1990) 'Computers in Social Intervention: Implications for Professional Social Work Practice and Education', *Family Therapy* 17/2: 109-121.

Pardeck, John T./Collier Umfress, Karen/Murphy, John W. (1987) 'The Use and Perception of Computers by Professional Social Workers', *Family Therapy* 14/1: 1-8.

Pardeck, John T./Collier Umfress, Karen/Murphy, John W. (1990) 'The Utilization of Computers on Social Service Agencies', pp. 121-128 in Pardeck, John T./Murphy, John W. (eds.) *Computers in Human Services: An Overview for Clinical and Welfare Services*. Chur: Harwood Academic Publishers.

Pardes, Y. (1977) *An Equation for Determining Community Worker Positions in Local Authorities*. Ramat Gan, Israel: Bar Ilan University Press (in Hebrew).

Pardes, Y. (1978). *A Method for Determining Social Worker Positions in the Social Services*. Jerusalem: Israel Ministry of Labour and Social Affairs (in Hebrew).

Parsloe, Phyllida (1989) 'An Example of Serendipity: the Unintended Impact of Computers on Social Work Practice', pp. 169-185 in Cnaan, Ram A./Parsloe, Phyllida (eds.) *The Impact of Information Technology on Social Work Practice*. New York: Haworth Press.

Parsons, H.M. (1985) 'Automation and the Individual: Comprehensive and Comparative Views', *Human Factors* 27: 99-112.

Parsons, Ruth J. (1991) 'Empowerment: Purpose and Practice Principle in Social Work', *Social Work with Groups* 14/2: 7-21.

Parsons, Talcott (1956) 'Suggestions for a Sociological Approach to a Theory of Organisations – 1', *Administrative Science Quarterly* 1: 63-85.

Penzias, Arno A. (1993) 'Information Technology Applications, Productivity in Human Services', pp. 17-28 in Leiderman, Marcos/Guzetta, Charles/Struminger, Leny/ Monnickendam, Menachem (eds.) *Technology in People Services: Research, Theory and Applications*. New York: Haworth Press.

Phillips, Bruce A./Dimsdale, Bernard/Taft, Ethel (1981) 'An Information System for the Social Casework Agency: A Model and Case Study', *Administration in Social Work* 5/3-4: 129-144.

Phillips, David (ed.) (1985a) *Programs in Practice: Register of Members' Interests*. Sheffield, Joint Unit for Social Services Research, University of Sheffield.

Phillips, David (1985b) 'Plans for PIP', *Programs in Practice Newsletter* 1: 1.

Phillips, David (1986a) 'Microcomputers as Aids to Social Work Practice', pp. 123-134 in Horobin, G./Montgomery, S. (eds.) *New Information Technology in Management and Practice*. Research Highlights in Social Work 13. London: Kogan Page.

Phillips, David (1986b) 'Clients Face to Face with Computers', *Community Care*, November, Supplement, i-iii.

Phillips, David (ed.) (1987) *Programs in Practice: Program, Catalogue*. Sheffield, Joint Unit for Social Services Research, University of Sheffield.

Phillips, David (1989) 'Human Services Computing: The State of the Art', *New Technology in the Human Services* 4/4: 23-32.

Phillips, David (1990) 'The Underdevelopment of Computing in Social Work Practice', *International Journal of Sociology and Social Policy* 10/4-6: 9-29

Phillips, David (1991a) 'Information Technology and the Human Services: Implications for Social Justice' *Computer Use in Social Services Network* 11/1-2: 34-35.

Phillips, David (1991b) *The Impact of New Technology on Social Work Practice*. Hong Kong Baptist College Occasional Paper Series, *4*, 1-17. Hong Kong.

Phillips, David (1993a) 'New Technology in the Human Services: Implications for Social Justice', pp. 465-477 in Leiderman, Marcos/Guzetta, Charles/Struminger, Leny/ Monnickendam, Menachem (eds.) *Technology in People Services: Research, Theory and Applications*. New York: Haworth Press.

Phillips, David (1993b) 'New Technology in the Human Services: Implications for Social Justice', *Computers in Human Services* 9/3-4: 465-477.

Poertner, John/Rapp, Charles A. (1987) 'Designing Social Work Management Information Systems: The Case for Performance Guidance Systems', *Administration in Social Work* 11/3-4: 177-190.

Pruger, Robert, (1986) 'Information Technology in Support of Service Delivery Decisions', pp. 212-227 in Geiss, Gunther R./Viswanathan, Narayan (eds.) *The Human Edge: Human Technology and Helping People*. New York: Haworth Press.

Radford, K. J. (1978) 'Some Initial Specifications for a Strategic Information System', *Omega* 6/2: 139-144.

Rapp, Charles A. (1984) 'Information, Performance and the Human Service Manager of the 1980's: Beyond 'Housekeeping'', *Administration in Social Work* 8/2: 69-80.

Reamer, Frederic G. (1986) 'The Use of Modern Technology in Social Work: Ethical Dilemmas', *Social Work* 31: 469-72.

Reinoehl, Richard/Brown, Helen/Iroff, Linda D. (1990) 'Computer Assisted Life Review', *Computers in Human Services* 6/1-3: 37-50.

Reinoehl, Richard/Hanna, Thomas (1990) 'Defining Computer Literacy in Human Services', *Computers in Human Services* 6/1-3: 3-20.

Reinoehl, Richard L./Mueller, B. Jeanne (1990) 'Introducing Computer Literacy in Human Service Education', *Computers in Human Services* 7/1-2: 3-15.

Reisman, Jane (1990) 'Gender Inequality in Computing', *Computers in Human Services* 7/1-2: 45-64.

Riley, Glenn M./Ickes, Steven J. (1989) 'Empowering Human Services Staff', pp. 277-286 in LaMendola, Walter/Glastonbury, Bryan/Toole, Stuart (eds.) *A Casebook of Computer Applications in the Social and Human Services*. New York: Haworth Press.

Romano, Mary D./Conklin, George S./Fisher, Dena (1985) 'Designing Information Systems for Hospital Social Work Management', *Computers in Human Services* 1/3: 47-58.

Rose, Richard (1976) 'Disciplined Research and Undisciplined Problems', *International Social Science Journal* 28/1: 99-121.

Ross, Murray G. (1967) *Community Organization: Theory, Principles, and Practice*. Harper and Row: New York.

Rowe, Christopher (1986) *People and Chips: the Human Implications of Information Technology*. London: Paradigm Publishing.

Rowley, J. E. (1990) 'Guidelines on the Evaluation and Selection of Library Software Packages', *ASLIB Proceedings* 42/9: 225-235.

Sainsbury, Eric (1977) *The Personal Social Services*. London: Pitman.

Saleebey, Dennis (1991) 'Technological Fix: Altering the Consciousness of the Social Work Profession', *Journal of Sociology and Social Welfare* 18/4: 51-67.

Sandhu, Jim Singh/Richardson, Steve (1988) *Concerned Technology 1989*. Newcastle, Handicapped Persons Research Unit, Newcastle-Upon-Tyne Polytechnic.

Schoech, Dick (1979) 'A Microcomputer Based Human Service Information System', *Administration in Social Work* 3/4: 423-440.

Schoech, Dick J. (1982) *Computer Use in Social Services*. New York: Human Sciences Press.

Schoech, Dick J. (1990) *Human Service Computing: Concepts and Applications*. New York: Haworth Press.

Schoech, Dick/Arangio, Tony (1979) 'Computers in Human Services', *Social Work* 24/2: 96-102.

Schoech, Dick/Jennings, Hal/Schkade, Lawrence L./Hooper-Russell, Chrisan (1985) 'Expert Systems: Artificial Intelligence for Professional Decisions', *Computers in Human Services* 1/1: 81-115.

Schoech, Dick J./Schkade, Lawrence L. (1980a) 'What Human Services Can Learn from Business about Computerization', *Public Welfare* 38/3: 18-27.

Schoech, Dick J./Schkade, Lawrence L. (1980b) 'Computers Helping Caseworkers: Decision Support Systems' *Child Welfare* 59/9: 566-575.

Schoech, Dick J./Schkade, Lawrence L./Sanchez Mayers, Raymond (1981) 'Strategies for Information System Development', *Administration in Social Work* 51/3-4: 11-26.

Schuerman, John R. (1987) 'Expert Consulting Systems in Social Welfare', *Social Work Research and Abstracts* 23/3: 14-18.

Schuerman, John R./Vogel, Lynn Harold (1986) 'Computer Support of Placement Planning: The Use of Expert Systems in Child Welfare', *Child Welfare* 65/6: 531-543.

Schwab Jr., A. James/Wilson, Susan S. (1990) 'Computer Literacy in Social Work: The Case for a Programming Language', *Computers in Human Services* 7/1-2: 77-94.

Senner, Les/Young, Barry G./Gunn, S. Richard/Schwartz, Charles L. (1988) 'Computer Use in the Human Services', *Computers in Human Services* 3/3-4: 101-110.

Shangraw, Ralph F. (1986) 'How Managers Use Information: An Experiment Examining Choices of Computer and Printed Information', *Public Administration Review* 46: 506-515.

Shapira, Monica (1981) *A Study of Information Utilisation in Disposition Assignments of Probation Officers*. Jerusalem, Hebrew University (in Hebrew).

Shapira, Monica, (1990) 'Computerised Decision Technology in Social Service: Decision Support System Improves Decision Practice in Youth Probation Service', *International Journal of Sociology and Social Policy* 10/4-6: 138-153.

Shapira, Monica/Levi, Jocelyn (1990) 'Users' Satisfaction', unpublished paper submitted to A.J.D.C., October 1990.

Sharkey, Peter (1989) 'Introducing Computing on a Social Work Course', *New Technology in the Human Services* 4/2: 3-6.

Silverman, David (1970) *The Theory of Organisations*. London: Heinemann Educational Books.

Simon, Herbert (1960) *The New Science of Management Decision*. New York: Harper and Row.

Simon, Herbert (1973) 'Applying Information Technology to Organization Design', *Public Administration Review* 33: 268-278.

Sircar, Sumit/Schkade, Lawrence L./Schoech, Dick (1983) 'The Data Base Management System Alternative for Computing in the Human Services', *Administration in Social Work* 7/1: 267-275.

Smith, N. J. (1985) *Social Welfare and Computers*. Melbourne: Longmans Cheshire.

Smith, Norman J./Bolitho, Floyd H. (1989) 'Information: The Hydra-Headed Concept in the Human Services', *Computers in Human Services* 5/3-4: 83-98.

Sonsel, George E./Paradise, Frank/Stroup, Stephen (1988) 'Case Management Practice in an AIDS Service Organization', *Social Casework* 69/6: 388-392.

Sprague, R. H./Carlson, E. D. (1982) *Building Effective Decision Support Systems*. Englewood Cliffs, NJ: Prentice Hall.

State Reorganization Commission (1989) *An Evaluation of the Human Services Integration Project*. Columbia: South Carolina State Reorganization Commission.

Steyaert, Jan (1992) 'Databases and Information Systems in Human Services: Where Do We Go From Here?', *New Technology in the Human Services* 6/1: 20-29.

Streatfield, David (1992) 'The Computer Minefield', *Community Care, Inside Information Technology Supplement,* 30 January: 1.

Stretch, John J. (1967) 'Existentialism: A Proposed Philosophical Orientation for Social Work', *Social Work* 12/4: 97-102.

Sullivan, Richard J. (1980) 'Human Issues in Computerized Social Services', *Child Welfare* 59/7: 401-406.

Swanson, E. B. (1978) 'The Two Faces of Organizational Information', *Accounting, Organizations and Society* 3: 237-246.

Taylor, J. B. (1981) *Using Micro-Computers in Social Agencies, Sage Services Guide 19*. Beverly Hills: Sage.

Torre, D. (1985) *Empowerment: Structured Conceptualization and Instrument Development*. New York, PhD dissertation, Cornell University, New York.

Turem, Jerry S. (1986) 'Social Work Administration and Modern Management Technology', *Administration in Social Work* 10/3: 15-24.

Vafeas, John G. (1991) 'Personal Computer Based Clinical Systems: A Goal Oriented Case Management Model', *Computers in Human Services* 8/2: 21-36.

Vallee, Jacques, (1986) 'The Network Revolution: Promises and Pitfalls in the Use of Information Technology', pp. 52-71 in Geiss, Gunther R./Viswanathan, Narayan (eds.) *The Human Edge: Human Technology and Helping People*. New York: Haworth Press.

van Hove, Erik, A. (1989) 'Three Lessons from Automating Social Services in Belgium', *New Technology in the Human Services* 4/2: 10-14.

Velasquez, Joan S./Lynch, Mary M. (1981) 'Computerized Information Systems: A Practice Orientation', *Administration in Social Work* 5/3-4: 113-127.

Vogel, Lynn Harold (1985) 'Decision Support Systems in the Human Services', *Computers in Human Services* 1/1: 67-80.

Wagman, Morton/Kerber, Kenneth (1980) 'PLATO-DCS. An Interactive Computer System for Personal Counselling: Further Development and Evaluation', *Journal of Counseling Psychology* 27: 31-39.

Wagner, Roland, M. (1987) 'Computer Usage by Social Services Agencies in Santa Clara County, California', *Computers in Human Services* 2/1-2: 79-84.

Wakefield, Rowan A. (1985) 'Computers, Family Empowerment and the Psychotherapist: Conceptual Overview and Outlook', pp. 9-20 in Figley, Charles R. (ed.) *Computers and Family Therapy*. New York: Haworth Press.

Watson, David (1989) 'Computers, Confidentiality and Privation', pp. 153-168 in Cnaan, Ram A./Parsloe, Phyllida (eds.) *The Impact of Information Technology on Social Work Practice*. New York: Haworth Press.

Webb, A. L./Wistow, G. (1986) *Planning, Need and Scarcity: Essays on the Personal Social Services*. London: Allen and Unwin.

Weber, Max (1964) *The Theory of Social and Economic Organisation*. New York: Free Press.

Weick, Ann (1987) 'Reconceptualizing the Philosophical Perspective of Social Work', *Social Service Review* 61/2: 218-230.

Weil, Marie/Karls, James M. and Associates (1985) *Case Management in Human Service Practice*. San Francisco: Jossey-Bass.

Weiss, C. H./Bucuvalas, M. J. (1980) 'Truth Tests and Utility Tests: Decision-Makers' Frames of Reference for Social Science Research', *American Sociological Review* 45: 302-313.

Weizenbaum, Joseph, (1976) *Computer Power and Human Reason: From Judgement to Calculation*. San Francisco: Freeman.

Williams, Sandra/Forrest, Jan (1988) 'Technology on Trial', pp. 214-222 in Glastonbury, Bryan/LaMendola, Walter/Toole, Stuart (eds.) *Information Technology and the Human Services*. Chichester: Wiley.

Wilson, John (1989) 'High Technology and Social Services', pp. 48-69 in Spence, W. R. (ed.) *New Technologies and Social Intervention*. Jordanstown, Northern Ireland: University of Ulster.

Wimberly, Edward T./Blazyk, Stan (1989) 'Monitoring Patient Outcome Following Discharge: A Computerized Geriatric Case Management System', *Health and Social Work* 14/4: 269-276.

Witkin, Stanley L./Gottschalk, Shimon (1989) 'Considerations in the Development of a Scientific Social Work', *Journal of Sociology and Social Welfare* 16/1: 19-29.

Wodarski, John S. (1988) 'Development of Management Information Systems for Human Services: A Practical Guide', *Computers in Human Services* 3/1-2: 37-49.